Arnold Schwarzenegger

Arnold Schwarzenegger

A Life on Film

ADRIAN WRIGHT

ROBERT HALE · LONDON

© Adrian Wright 1994
First published in Great Britain 1994

ISBN 0 7090 5053 4

Robert Hale Ltd
Clerkenwell House
Clerkenwell Green
London EC1R 0HT

2   4   6   8   10   9   7   5   3   1

Set in Monotype Ehrhardt by Bookcraft, Stroud, Gloucestershire
Printed in Great Britain by St Edmundsbury Press,
Bury St Edmunds, Suffolk
and bound by WBC Bookbinders

Contents

Illustrations

All illustrations courtesy of the British Film Institute

For Janet

Introduction

Why another book about Arnold Schwarzenegger?

For any author starting out on a biography, there has to be a good reason to concentrate on the life and work of another person for a part of his or her life. If someone else has been there before, turned the handle of the moviola and spilled the beans, what point is there in going over worked ground, paraphrasing what other biographers and countless journalists have already written? My first task, when contemplating a life of Arnold Schwarzenegger, was to spread out what had gone before. Had someone else already written the book I intended to write?

Unless it is to be a thing of absolute dreariness, any biography must be more than a mere bringing together of known facts about its subject. A viewpoint helps – no matter what it is; an opinion shared between the biographer and reader is comforting, an opinion offered by the biographer and violently rejected by the reader is stimulating. It is not necessary to agree with everything a writer says about his subject; it is often much healthier to disagree with it. A biography is a journey through a life, and the writer's understanding of his subject develops and shifts as the writing proceeds. For the writer, as well as the reader, it is a learning process.

The life of a film actor, and particularly of a living film actor, is often characterized by a distinction between 'the myth and the man'. Both are a problem to the biographer. The myth is probably the most dangerous, not least because it usually attempts to convince us that it is the man. In truth, the myth is made up of various elements. For most of us, film actors live mainly in what we see on the screen. For the space of two hours, the most obnoxious individual in Hollywood can move us to tears playing the world's greatest philanthropist. This would come under the heading of myth, and the publicity and hype forming a backdrop to the actor often contributes to the reinforcement and acceptance of such myth, though perhaps less so since the days when movie-goers were so gullible that every silly titbit engineered into the gossip pages of film magazines was gobbled up unquestioningly.

A real understanding of the man, as distinct from the myth, is even harder. It is not always easy to understand ourselves, let alone one another. The biographer worth his salt can only present the facts and try to understand them, looking at his subject sympathetically but critically.

The distinction between myth and man can be a chasm, yet the myth often informs us of the man. In the case of any creative artist we must believe this, because our understanding of that artist relies to a great extent on the work he puts before us. This book's subtitle – A Life on Film – betrays my conviction that much of the subject's life is lived out in his work.

The fact that my other biographies of film actors – Sylvester Stallone and Kevin Costner – have sailed under the same subtitle does not mean that I have twisted my understanding of their lives into some mythical reworking on film. What we see on screen is acting, acting that began with an idea, developed into writing, and has been directed into the framework of a movie. Wherever that idea began, and no matter what forces helped transmute it into what struggled into the light of day, it is essential that we see its place in the subject's life. Those books already written about Arnold Schwarzenegger do not always fall in line with this theory, but a careful examination of them – each superimposed on the other – reveals the territory that has been adequately covered.

Wendy Leigh's *Arnold* (1990), unauthorized as it is, can claim to be the only full biography to date, taking in the whole of Arnold's life and presenting a relentlessly critical look at his personal life. Miss Leigh's well-researched facts rub along beside dark suggestions of disloyalty, opportunism, brute determination and the existence of several cupboards of skeletons, among them the child's ex-Nazi parentage.

She also seems not to be particularly interested in how Arnold earns his money, for his movies are not given much space in her account – unsurprisingly, for an expansive discussion of them would be of little point in what is essentially a one-dimensional attempt at character assassination. A jester at the wedding Miss Leigh is definitely not. Her author's note is as intriguing as anything in the actual body of the text, with its final acknowledgement to 'the best libel lawyers any author could ever hope for'.

More modestly, Brooks Robards' *Arnold Schwarzenegger* (1992) is a sketchy but no-nonsense progress through the life and movies, its slender but well-prepared narrative adding some weight to a generous collection of glossily attractive photographs. Even slimmer, K.W. Woods' *Schwarzenegger: Muscleman to Terminator* (1991) skips through the life in six pages and moves briskly on to a movie-by-movie format with sixty pages looking at 'the movies, the muscle and the man'.

Far and away the best book to have been written is *Arnold Schwarzenegger: A Portrait* by George Butler (1990). It is a remarkable document. Promoted as 'the true story behind the making of a champion', it deals only with Arnold's career as a body-builder, charted by Butler's excellent prose and superb photographs. Every picture tells its story, and Butler seems always to have been watching his subject at a revealing moment.

The images tumble over one another as we turn these pages. Here is Arnold sitting in class at a Santa Monica evening school, the will to better himself marking him out from the fellow students around him; here is Arnold in the agony of extreme physical training; here is Arnold, his happiness signposted by his gappy smile, his sexual prowess the attention of a clutch of young South African boys, bikini-clad girls lazing on a beach, or a pair of admiring grannies on a park bench. Here we see Arnold with his mother in a handful of informal shots that show us so much of their relationship. For anyone wanting to understand Schwarzenegger, Butler's highly intelligent book is indispensable. Schwarzenegger's final reaction to the book his friend had written about him – the conversation recalled by Butler in the closing pages – enriches our understanding of him.

And so to the present biography, in which I have tried to gain a proper perspective on Schwarzenegger's life and work – an evaluation rather than an exposé, an offering of viewpoints and opinions rather than a definitive statement. The absolute definition of any biographical subject cannot be successfully managed until the subject's death - and even then there is no guarantee that a biographer can bring it off.

The reverberations of Schwarzenegger's successes test our perception and understanding, for failure seems to have played very little part in his life; it is as if he simply refused to court it. The result of his achievements, in both the personal and professional spheres, appears to be unassailable, and there is no whisper of any possible dethronement.

As Sylvester Stallone (once Schwarzenegger's arch-rival) watched his career go down the drain he allowed Schwarzenegger to move into that special first place in Hollywood that had once, briefly, been Stallone's own. Schwarzenegger's tenancy as the cinema's pre-eminent muscle-action-hero is certain to be much longer, for his grip on his craft, his understanding of what he has to offer and who he is selling it to, marks him out as a consummate professional and Stallone as a hopeful amateur. Those whom Schwarzenegger once emulated and looked to – among them Steve Reeves, the deposed body beautiful of Hollywood and international movie adventures of classical derring-do – are left behind as the gap between their success and his widens.

Schwarzenegger has brought many talents to his career. Beside the acumen he has showed in his professional life as an actor is the success he brought to his first career as a body-builder. There is also his political skill, coming together with the efficiency evident in the organization of his well-ordered home and business life. It is not only the manner in which Schwarzenegger moved beyond the boundaries marked out in the film industry for ex-musclemen, but the excellence of so much of his work, that is so often overlooked.

Just as his technical armoury has progressed from the rawness of his early work to what is never less than perfect competence, Schwarzenegger's screen persona has clearly developed and changed. Like Burt Lancaster, another splendid physique who might have been expected to trade his body for his career, Schwarzenegger's passion for excellence has been learned the hard way, through aiming for the top in everything — and succeeding.

1 Kicking Ass

Thal, a small village a few miles from the capital of Styria in Austria, has always kept its long history to itself. The churches of St Korbinian, built on a hill overlooking the valley, and of St Ulrich, have stood since the fifteenth century. The church of St Korbinian, with its three fine side altars, a high altar dating from 1660, and a fifteenth century Madonna, has often provided refuge in troubled times. For two hundred years, between 1469 and 1683, Styria was threatened by the Turks, standing as it did on the edge of the Holy Roman Empire.

Close to Thal is Graz, the second largest city in Austria, spread out along the banks of the Mur River. When the Turks no longer proved a threat, Napoleon occupied the city on three different occasions; the fact that Graz reminds so many visitors of Vienna may only have been one of the reasons for his persistent interest.

Thal's attractions may have been less sophisticated than those of Graz, but it was here that Aurelia Schwarzenegger gave birth to her first child on 17 July 1946. A son, he was called Meinhard, though the more homely 'Meinhardl' was soon in common use around the home. The following year, on 30 July, a second boy was born to Aurelia and Gustav Schwarzenegger. His given name, Arnold, was of German origin, meaning 'eagle-power', a promising beginning for a child born under the aegis of Leo, whose children are supposed to be extroverts, stubborn leaders, and blessed with the luck of the devil. As for the surname, an offered translation of Schwarzenegger, 'blackploughman', suggests a determined strength that is not altogether out of character.

The Schwarzeneggers were a hard-working, working-class,

uncomplicated family, rooted in the steel industries of Neuberg. Gustav, Arnold's father, was one of four children born to Karl and Cecilia Schwarzenegger. Karl's strong physique suggested that he was well able to cope with the heavy physical demands of his work but, following an accident, he died while still a young man, leaving Cecilia to live to be over eighty years old.

As a young man, Gustav had been expected to work in the industry that had employed his father and other Schwarzenegger men before him, but he went on to join the Austrian army, balancing his militaristic interests with his strong Catholicism. When they were children, Arnold and Meinhard were expected to accompany their parents to Sunday church services. Gustav had other interests, among which was music. He played several musical instruments, including the flugelhorn, well enough for him to be incorporated into the Graz Gendarmerie Musik, with which he remained associated throughout his life. In his well-ordered life, Gustav then decided to join the police force, and did well, rising to a senior position, a respected figure made more important by his parochial setting.

Gustav met and fell in love with Aurelia Jadrny towards the end of the Second World War. Born in Styria in 1922, Aurelia was fifteen years younger than her lover, and had already survived a marriage with a Herr Barmuller. 'Reli', as Aurelia was affectionately nicknamed by Gustav, succumbed to the handsomeness of her new suitor, and the pair were married on 20 October 1945. Gustav's progress in the police force looked promising, and he was eventually posted as a Commandant to Thal. The job was probably not particularly demanding for a man of Gustav's ambition and determination, and the cessation of hostilities had put an end to another of his great interests, his membership of the Nazi Party, to which he pledged his allegiance on 4 July 1938. This time in his life was seldom discussed with Aurelia, who anyway thought it better not to dig too deeply. 'I don't suppose he ever said more than a few words to me about the war or what he did in it in the 27 years that we were married,' she said.

Nevertheless, accusations of a possible zest for his duties have sometimes shadowed those who survived Gustav, with Arnold experiencing the father's sins being visited on the son. Wendy Leigh's biography suggests that Gustav may indeed have played an active role in the Nazi Party, and Arnold's mind was certainly exercised enough to undertake some private research at the Simon Wiesenthal Centre to see if any evidence of his father's activities could be unearthed.

The Schwarzenegger's home at 145 Thal-Linak was less comfortable than might be expected of the abode of a reasonably paid police chief, though the accommodation had been specifically intended for the holder of the post. Supposedly built by the Austrian royal family some 300 years before, the downstairs quarters were reserved for the current forest ranger, the upstairs for the Chief of Police.

The conditions verged on the primitive. Water had to be fetched from an outside source, there was no inside lavatory, no refrigerator and no telephone. Heating was at a premium. Such post-war austerity probably suited Gustav's temperament, ill-suited as it was to unbridled comfort. Occasionally he seemed to mistake the family home for a barracks, leading his own life along well-ordered lines and expecting his wife and sons to follow the example. Aurelia in the main responded to his influence, providing a spotlessly clean, strictly timetabled environment for her family.

'You could eat off the floors,' said Arnold many years later. 'The towels would have sharp corners when they were folded and stacked up. The household was a full-time occupation. I have one of the best mothers anybody could have.'

Arnold also had a fondness for his father, though the fondness seems to have been more guarded. In every sense Gustav was happy to be the father figure, the god figure, needing to be satisfied or assuaged, seeing his role as setting demands and standards that must be met by those around him. Despite this formidable ability Arnold did not seem unduly intimidated, and always felt able to approach Gustav if a problem arose. If Gustav sometimes responded with a backlash, it was no more than might be expected of so dutiful a father. His need to see conformity and respectability all round him had its contradictory side. It was not unknown for him to come home to Aurelia after a heavy bout of drinking; indeed, she seems to have had to put up with a good deal of such behaviour over the years of their life together. When she was pregnant with Arnold, Gustav made her life unpleasant by suggesting he might not be the father of the child. Perhaps unsurprisingly, Gustav seems also not to have been specially popular with the men who worked alongside him. At home, he worked to instil the virtues he saw in himself in his sons, willing them to be the successful boys he wanted them to be.

Arnold did not seem dispirited by the domestic regime, made less easy by the fact that Meinhard was the obvious favourite of his parents. As the two boys developed, Gustav took pleasure in comparing their achievements and behaviour, a comparison from which Meinhard usually emerged the victor. Sharing a bedroom with his sibling meant that Arnold was fully exposed to Meinhard's shining qualities though, from early years, Arnold nursed the suspicion that his brother's star would not always be in the ascendant.

Childhood ailments and the tendency to get into trouble marked Arnold's progress through boyhood. High spirits and naughtiness might occasionally boil over into something more aggressive, though the stern paternal retribution waiting at home acted as an effective deterrent. There seem to have been few gaps in a normal day when a boy's spirit might ride free.

The Schwarzenegger household rose punctually at 6 a.m., at which hour Arnold and Meinhard would bustle about helping Aurelia with the various chores that got the Schwarzenegger home up and running for the day. The pursuit of pleasure was organized on fairly joyless lines, and might then be made the subject of a written essay prescribed by Gustav, who would stipulate the length of the work to be prepared and read through it carefully, correcting what mistakes he could identify.

Arnold's exposure to a world beyond the confines of this well-disciplined machine was limited. When he and Meinhard began attending the Hans Gross School in Thal, it is not surprising that they sometimes kicked against the reins of this new authority in their lives. The headmaster's attention was on more than one occasion drawn to their misconduct, though whether he told Gustav of such incidents is not known. School did have its good points, for the journey from home each morning gave Arnold living experience of

the macho world he would come to exemplify. Austria was still occupied by peacekeeping forces of the US Army, and Arnold rode to
school in a 40-millimetre cannoned truck. He quickly struck up a
friendship with the American soldiers, glimpsing in them some of
the experience he so badly wanted for himself.

Home increasingly came to mean little more than board and bed-
ding to him. Late at night, he would sometimes steal away from his
bedroom to the football stadium at Graz where he could begin
working on the physical improvement of his body. If the house
proved inaccessible on his return, he did not mind settling down to
sleep in a barn. When nightly escape from home became impossible, he extemporized with heating pipes and other household
fixtures that could be used as temporary body-building equipment.
Even as a boy, Arnold did not take happily to wasting time.

His earliest ambition, he remembered long after, was 'to go out
in the world with a hat, a stick and a monkey'. Meanwhile, sport
proved a consuming interest and, in Arnold's mind, was a crucial
stepping-stone to something beyond his childhood surroundings.
'From the age of ten,' he explained, 'I wanted to be the best. I
thought I had been born in the wrong country. All I wanted to do
was leave Austria and come to America, and when I got here I
would not be one of the masses.'

Such determination may not sound particularly arrogant in the
words of a ten-year-old who had no specific idea about how he
would rise above the masses he clearly deplored. A seed may have
been planted when, at the age of six, Arnold was taken by his father
into Graz to see the opening ceremony of a new swimming pool.
The city fathers had been inspired enough to hire a living embodiment of American health, glamour and success to mark the event:
Johnny Weissmuller. Here was an Olympic swimming champion
who had been elevated to stardom in Hollywood when in 1932 he
first put on the loincloth of Tarzan, the Ape Man, a bread-ticket he
carried until well into the 1940s, beyond which he sustained a career in
movies into the 1950s. Like other examples of manhood which
would appeal to Arnold, Weissmuller was proof that a brilliant body
could get a person noticed, and that all life was in America.

Gustav's fondest hope for Arnold was that he would become a

footballer or champion skier (Gustav having established himself as a championship ice-curler). At thirteen, although Arnold was proving himself on the soccer field, any success his team might win meant little to him; if he had been a singer, Arnold would never have enjoyed being in a choir — it was as a soloist that he would have wanted to succeed. Moving away from soccer, he seemed about to work his way through every sport under the sun when his tutor (a man who has a good deal to answer for) suggested some weightlifting exercises. They were Arnold's first steps along the road to his obsession, his *raison d'être*, his notoriety, and his claim to be counted as a unique creature of the twentieth century.

By the age of fifteen, the discipline Arnold exercised over his training was already ferocious, but everywhere he was surrounded by body-building fanatics who thrilled to watch the boy devoting more and more of his life to the glorification of his body. Beside this, Gustav's sporting accomplishments seemed small fry indeed, and Arnold's new-found independence through his body-building further distanced him from his father. This individualism came out in other ways, as when Arnold decided he did not need God. He decided that he could achieve anything he wanted on his own terms by his own effort, and informed his parents that his days of church-going were finished. Arnold no longer had to try to be the man his father wanted him to be; Gustav now had to appreciate the son Arnold had become.

Arnold recognized, even at this age, that working towards a perfect body brought the most diverse of sensations, pain and pleasure, and knew that elements of the one might be found in the other. As a teenager he was acutely aware of the sexual kicks his efforts at pumping his body gave him, weighing these against the physical suffering he inflicted on himself.

As a balm to these wounds, Arnold's sporting interests were balanced by the motion pictures he loved to see, where the gods of body-building were transmuted by the magic of light, costume, music and colour. Gazing up at the screen where Steve Reeves, Reg Park, Gordon Mitchell, Brad Harris or Mark Forrest starred, flexed their muscles and tried to act their way through some colourful epic, Arnold began piecing together his ambitions, and the plan needed to achieve them. The irony — for Reeves and Park and their like — is that, within only a few years, Arnold's achievement would far outstrip any they had managed.

Arnold seems to have preferred Park as his *alter ego* rather than Reeves, perhaps because Park had the more pronounced physique and was a bigger name in body-building, Reeves having given himself more wholeheartedly to the world of movies.

'He was the one I wanted to look like,' said Arnold of Park. 'His was the rugged physique, not the Steve Reeves pretty kind of thing. I saw [Park] in some Hercules movies, then I read about him in magazines. I started to look very much like him because when you lock yourself mentally into an image, your body starts shaping itself to it.'

As Arnold developed, and eventually beat Park in competition, his role models changed and Park was displaced, but in the early years both Park and Reeves had much to inspire the young Arnold, and their careers had walked many of the same paths that Arnold would tread.

He was not alone in taking notice of Steve Reeves. The good-looking, impressive one-time Mr Universe and Mr America first showed up on film as a supporting dude in the infamous director Edward D. Wood Jnr's almost unbelievably amateur *Jail Bait* (1954). This poverty row production, with its ludicrous tale of crooks and their molls wrapped up in a laughable plot about plastic surgery, has to be seen to be believed, as do Wood's other classic titles, including the wonderful *Plan 9 from Outer Space* (1956) and the little-seen *Glen or Glenda or I Changed my Sex* (1953), a searing but acutely funny shocker about transvestism, in which Wood himself was able to indulge one of his favourite pastimes, the wearing of angora sweaters.

By 1957 Reeves had established himself, playing Hercules in the first of many spectacular Italian-made epics, and quickly established himself as the (usually bearded) hero of many more mythological adventures, even if there was a constant rumour that his voice was dubbed to cover the high-pitched tones which might have contradicted his terrific physical presence. When Arnold compared Reeves to Park, Reeves proved the loser.

Park was always less of a star than Reeves, taking over where Reeves left off in the early sixties and making a speciality of playing Hercules, giving the public *Hercules in the Haunted World* (1961), *Hercules and the Captive Women* (1963) and *Hercules, Prisoner of Evil* (1964/67), all of which earned him a strong following at the box office.

The fact was that Park's directors and writers often came up with better films than had been built around Reeves, but by the mid-sixties re-runs of mythological muscle-bound heroics were beginning to pall with the public, who would soon be greeted by a host of Reeves lookalikes. If their acting ability was usually strictly limited, this seemed little handicap to their success. Arnold looked to them for inspiration, but it was Park's physique and attainment that filled Arnold's mind to the exclusion of everything else. He studied photographs of Park's fabulous body, the width of his chest, each detail of his pectorals, hoping to come closer to an understanding of how such massive physical superiority could be come by. His one overwhelming ambition was to grow to be like Park, and to have his body immortalized on film.

The inevitable marriage of a beautiful physique with a career in movies, where all might admire the body, had been planted in Arnold's mind. Gustav's reaction to all this was predictably dismissive: how could Arnold hope to transcend his culture and background in this way?

Arnold knew the answer to be in effort and yet more effort, and turned back to the barbell. If Arnold was to make his presence felt, he knew it would be a serious business. According to the bodybuilder Rick Wayne, by the age of thirteen Arnold was taking steroids, regularly injecting primobolin and popping dianabol tablets. He also began to get to know people who could influence his future.

In the early sixties, Arnold managed a meeting with no less a figure than Mr Austria, Kurt Marnul, who was so impressed by Arnold's enterprise and promise that he offered both Arnold and Meinhard the opportunity to train at his gymnasium, the Athletic Union, in Graz. Gustav must have looked on this with some anxiety, for this was not the sort of sporting ability he hoped to bring out in his sons. As if to prove the fact that he was not concerned with following in his father's footsteps, Arnold only managed to take sixth place in the 1962 ice-curling championship. He made himself the friend of a local politician, Alfred Gerstl, who welcomed Arnold into the heart of his family and into the well-appointed gymnasium he owned.

Meinhard's fortunes, after his beginnings as a prize son, had somewhat dimmed. His relationship with Gustav reflected many of the difficulties experienced by Arnold, and Meinhard's rebellious attitude to authority did not bode well. His behaviour at school eventually resulted in his being sent to a reformatory and, though Gustav retained hopes of a distinguished future for his elder son, Meinhard threw up his studies in 1962 and settled to a job with an electronics firm. At the back of his mind Arnold still carried the feeling that 'something' would one day happen to his brother, as well as an awareness that Meinhard had absorbed more than his fair share of his parents' love and attention. This concern spurred Arnold on to success even more, and helped to give him a brilliantly uncluttered view of his own future: 'I had a clear view of myself being on stage winning the Mr Universe contest, and I was driven by that thought. It was a very spiritual thing . . . it was a wonderful experience to be taken by a higher force and just led there.'

2   Born to Ambition

In 1962 Gustav was moved to a new post at the police station in Raaba, safely beyond Graz. This was not a promotion and it seems likely (according to Leigh) that an unprofessional incident involving the pestering of a woman on a bus led to Gustav being discreetly moved away from the relative prominence of Graz. Such a change cannot have pleased Aurelia or her sons, and Gustav was not the sort of father who could be consoled or helped through such a trauma.

'There was a wall,' Arnold said of their relationship. 'He established that wall. In America, parents want to be the child's friend, whereas my father had no patience for that.'

Like Meinhard, Arnold had to put childhood behind him and face the reality of earning a living. At the age of fifteen he started out on a three-year apprenticeship with a firm in Graz that specialized in making building materials, at a starting salary of 250 schillings a month for his first year. Perhaps to break the threatening monotony of such a career, he finally pleased Gustav by coming first in the national junior ice-curling championship in the spring of 1964, when, by a happy coincidence, Gustav was named as national adult ice-curling champion. As Arnold left adolescence, his relationship with Gustav seems to have settled into something quite amicable, if not especially close, as Arnold's interests in building up his body began to consume his every moment. 'My father supported me in everything I did,' said Arnold. 'It's just that he didn't understand about the body-building. It's not really an Austrian thing.'

On 1 October 1965, at the age of eighteen, Arnold was conscripted for the regulation one-year period into the Austrian army, where his background of home discipline at least proved useful. Arnold found this period stimulating, responding to the masculine environment, the militarism, the uniforms and medals, and was taken on as a tank driver despite the fact that he was too young for the job. This degree of favour was not enough for him, however, when he received an invitation to enter himself as a candidate in the Junior Mr Europe contest of 30 October 1965. Knowing he would not be granted permission to attend, Arnold slipped away from camp and made the journey to Stuttgart.

It was an auspicious beginning for Arnold, made memorable by his first meeting with the diminutive Sardinian body-builder, Franco Columbu, henceforth one of Arnold's greatest friends and friendliest opponents. Even the never immodest Arnold could tell that Franco, though built on a small scale (only 5'5"), was perfectly formed, and certainly the better-looking of the two men. Franco's ambition, however, lacked the biting edge of Arnold's, which may also have made him attractive to Arnold. At Stuttgart, when it came for the moment of judgement, Arnold's presentation was heavily based on everything he had ever seen Reg Park do, but Arnold won, beginning a decade in which he would gather up every trophy his sport had to offer.

Meanwhile the Army awaited the return of its temporary deserter and, while a sort of punishment was meted out, there was a general feeling that Arnold was returning to the service as a hero, his reputation enhanced. Arnold must now have realized that a career had been well and truly put in motion, and was greatly encouraged by his meeting with two other men who had been impressed by his performance at Stuttgart. One was the gay publisher and gymnasium-owner Rolf Putziger (who, awed as he was by Arnold's prowess, laughed when Arnold told him his next intention was to become Mr Universe), the other a guru of British body-building, Wag Bennett. Both made noises to Arnold about his heady future in the sport, but for the moment Arnold had to work out the remainder of his army days, now made more comfortable by the authorities who obligingly made physical training a heavy part of his regime. His fanatical discipline showed no sign of weakening as Arnold worked out for up to six hours at a stretch.

Putziger's offer of a job in his Munich gymnasium held good when Arnold was discharged, and he began work there in August 1966. He accepted Putziger's invitation to move into his house – a comfortable base and a considerable saving to Arnold on his living expenses. As trainer at the gymnasium, Arnold was at once satisfied and frustrated – satisfied that he could use the facilities around him, but frustrated at having to spend so many hours of every day trying to pass a few crumbs of his genius on to lesser mortals. For such an egotist as Arnold this must have been an exhausting time: he spoke of his clients' efforts as 'disgusting' and 'superficial'. The demands of paying customers did, however, have one advantage apart from keeping him in work: they meant that Arnold had to devise a split schedule of training, whereby he could utilize the hours in which he wasn't pestered by others. For two hours in the early morning he would work on his shoulders and arms, and in the evening concentrate on developing his chest, abdomen and legs.

His home life, too, proved unsatisfactory, and he complained to Putziger about his cramped accommodation. Putziger invited him to share his own comfortable bed, but Arnold was neither naïve enough to be shocked or gullible enough to accept the offer. He realized that homosexuality played its part in the body-building world, but resisted Putziger's vision of a life of easy success, and left to find his own place, compensated by the fact that Putziger had not been paying him a king's ransom of a salary.

Since winning the Junior Mr Europe title, Arnold's vision had intensified until there was no doubt in his mind that the Junior would soon drop from his title. That had been only a beginning; soon he would go on to become Mr Universe. By 1975 it was obvious that, at least as far as body-building was concerned, Arnold had effectively taken over every title that might be won. Mr Europe, Mr Universe, Mr World and (the Grecian title to crown them all) Mr Olympia, offered crowns of glory from which only a second gnawing ambition – to be in films – would force an abdication.

Arnold has always needed heroes. In his body-building days he looked back beyond the Reg Parks and Steve Reeves to a man whose legendary strength strode the nineteenth century: Eugene ('The

Great') Sandow. At a time when cinema was in its infancy, Sandow recognized that the presentation of his powerful physique was showbiz at its most basic. In the 1920s he appeared with a circus, making $2,000 a week from his nightly presentations. He was handsome, ambitious and acquisitive, certainly of women, who responded to his tight curly blond hair, his musculature and his fame. The end of his life also probably held a warning for Arnold, for Sandow crashed his car, lifted it to rescue a friend trapped underneath, and suffered a heart attack from which he subsequently died. Sandow, Park, Reeves – all reputations and names that had to be lived up to.

It was a case of getting his name known, and Arnold was never the shrinking violet of body-building. It was not simply a sport to him, but a philosophy, an intellectual need to understand the possibilities of the male body. It was also intellectual, in so much as Arnold saw it as mind as well as matter; his strength began in his mind. 'The concentration when I'm training,' he explained, 'means that I'm almost mentally inside the muscle. That's the ultimate. The physical thing is what you see first, but to get to that stage the mind is much more important.'

In September 1966 the National Amateur Body Builders Association Mr Universe competition was held at the Victoria Palace Theatre, London, and Arnold, of course, was there, determined to win the title. It was not to be. The new Mr Universe was Chet Yorton, an American superstar of the sport who had made a vague attempt at film stardom by making a movie with fellow bodybuilder Dave Draper, *Don't Make Waves*.

Coming second would have been enough for some competitive spirits, but not for Arnold, who nevertheless realized, as he watched Yorton compete and pose, how much he still had to absorb and learn. No matter that Arnold's arrival in London had been greeted with something like hysteria – after all, he was a pretty remarkable specimen for a boy of his age – Arnold was still a pretender to the throne of body-building, his gauche and unworldly attitudes on full display (this was the first time, for example, he had ever seen 'blacks with frizzy hair'). It was one thing for Arnold to tell everybody who would listen in London that he was going to be a great star and make a million bucks, but silently he understood that much work had to be done, not least a more professional attitude to his body-building. New friends were made who would influence and promote Arnold's future. Wag Bennett assured Arnold that, in his opinion, it was Yorton who should have been placed second. Coming from a man who knew, worked with, and had lived with Reg Park, Arnold sat up and took notice, telling Bennett of his huge ambitions. Bennett and his wife Dianne took Arnold under their wing, taking him to their gym in Forest Gate and admitting him into their own family. It was Bennett who taught Arnold that body-building is show-business, that a wonderful body is simply the beginning. Arnold posed to the music that Bennett suggested, and the inspiring surges of 'Exodus' encouraged him to ever greater exhibitions in London, Holland and Belgium.

Returning to the gym in Munich, Arnold was greeted by celebrations dampened by his parents' continuing lack of understanding. His independence strengthened when the opportunity arose for Arnold to purchase the gym he had been working in, and he seized the chance, working even harder to pay back the loans he had borrowed. Through the power of his own name he was able to double the number of clients at the gym. Progress, though slow, was being made, as Arnold increasingly grew apart from his Austrian roots.

'Everything I wanted as a kid was American,' he said. 'I hated everything about Austria – the classical music and the museums. I hated this old shit. Austrian films always dealt with the Alps and the hunter falling in love with some yo-yo girl in the forest and the farm. As soon as I saw that, I was gone!'

3 Boom, Boom, Boom

For the moment, the idea of appearing in films was a far distant thought. 1966 was a crowded year, bringing Arnold much success, including Best Built Man of Europe, the International Powerlifting Championship and the title of Mr Europe. When, in 1967, he won the amateur Mr Universe title in Great Britain, Arnold's arrival could not be ignored. Reg Park consolidated Arnold's achievement by asking him to spend that Christmas with him and his wife in Johannesburg, an irresistible accolade for the twenty-year-old.

Arnold's first conversation with his boyhood hero was stilted and awkward, not least because Arnold's grasp of English was still unsteady, but a friendship was nevertheless struck, and Park made it known that he saw a successor in Arnold. Quite how this would happen seemed unclear.

Life back in Munich was proving difficult. Arnold was getting into trouble with the police over fights and driving fast cars badly, while still being starved of the parental approval he yearned for. The winning of the Mr Universe title (Arnold beating the favourite to win, Dennis Tinnerino) widened the gap between Arnold's home life and his international career, as he hoped it would. Arnold's strategy seemed simple enough: his determination and will to come top of the heap were as important as any physical attributes he brought to the contest. He constantly wrote down that he was going to be a winner. The fact that he had won was clouded by the fact that there were in fact four different Mr Universe titles, of which he had won only one, but the victory was considerable.

It was now that another powerful manipulator in the body-building world – Joe Weider – began his association with Arnold.

Twenty-five years Arnold's senior, Joe, with his brother Ben, was a colossus of the body-building fraternity, through the International Federation of Body Building and the various body-building magazines that Weider published for followers and practitioners of the sport, magazines that had themselves given hope and inspiration to the young Arnold. The Weiders, too, had claimed responsibility for discovering no less than Reg Park, and Arnold could have wanted no more guarantee of their worth.

Joe immediately saw Arnold's potential and invited him to come to the USA, where Joe would promote his career, paying Arnold a salary so that he could train and improve, and at the same time use Arnold's growing name as a figurehead for product promotions and magazine articles. For the moment Arnold bided his time, returning to Munich and the gym and a growing friendship with Franco Columbu, but there could be no doubt that Arnold's ultimate ambitions lay exactly where Joe and his brother pointed – the land of great white hope, America.

Meanwhile, Johannesburg and Reg Park's palatial starry home beckoned, with Arnold at last visiting the star he had idolized and modelled himself on for so many years. A picture of them rising, like two Titans, from Park's Olympic-sized swimming pool, is remarkable. The two men dwarf the pool, their massive bodies rising triumphant from the depths; if we did not know otherwise we might think the picture was a moment from a Ray Harryhausen special effect.

By now, Arnold's confidence had greatly improved, and he was impressed by the milieu he found himself in. He saw how Park's success and wealth had lead to a glamorous lifestyle of gathered antiques, of servants ready to serve (the fact that this was South Africa might not have occurred to the young Arnold as an explanation of the latter). What he experienced during his time with Park certainly showed Arnold the value of a movie actor's currency, and he liked what he saw. As for being an actor himself, anything remotely close to such a thing still seemed remote. As Arnold was to admit after his first movie appearances: 'I was told many times that . . . my name was a stumbling block. I was told that my body was a stumbling block. But I learned with body-building that anything can be accomplished if you are willing to take the sacrifices and if you're willing to work for it. I never really felt that I was wasting my time. I had all the time in the world.'

Back in Munich, he redoubled his efforts to build up business at the gym, and turned to even more strenuous training, meaning to take the professional NABBA Mr Universe title in London in 1968. He did so, and Joe Weider encouraged Arnold to spread his wings and compete in the IFBB version of the Mr Universe contest in Miami, Florida, in late September 1968. Arnold made the journey, filled with confidence, only to watch Frank Zane take the title. Arnold had perhaps been a little blasé after his recent triumphs, was almost certainly not in the condition he needed to be in, and was not yet equipped with the physical requisites of American body-building. At a time when Joe's hold on Arnold's career was tightening, this failure must have strengthened Joe's position as mentor and controller, as well as teaching Arnold about the art of losing. It was a humiliating blow for Arnold, but he intended it to be only a temporary setback; lessons would be learned, and America was probably the place to learn the hardest lessons.

Under an agreement he made with Joe, Arnold agreed to spend a year in the United States, at the same time keeping on his Munich business interests. Arnold was learning something from Joe's wily business acumen, as well as adapting his Austrian mentality to the material pressures of American life.

1968 brought other conquests, the German Powerlifting Championship and the IFBB Mr International in Mexico, but it was the American influences that were having most effect on Arnold. He loved what America offered after the constriction of Austria, and blossomed in the California sun, taking a small apartment in Santa Monica, training for a time with Vince Gironda before moving on to Gold's Gym in Venice, a Mecca of body-builders and an institution with which Arnold would become solidly identified. It became the centre of his world, a world over which he ruled, held in awe by aspiring body-builders and proved champions alike.

Any hatchet that had existed between Arnold and Frank Zane was buried when he asked Zane to teach him mathematics. When they were not exploring the wonders of algebra they talked about body-building, a sport Arnold seemed intent on taking over when in 1969 he secured two more Mr Universe titles, in the amateur US contest and the professional British contest. This was the year when both Arnold and his admirers recognized that he had reached a peak of bodily perfection; he spoke of getting his body down from an animal mass of flesh to a work of art. It was also the year when a woman other than Aurelia came to offer him more than a passing gratification.

A steady, homely, blonde, twenty-year-old girl working as a Santa Monica waitress to pay her way through teacher training may not have seemed likely as a serious partner for the upwardly mobile Arnold, but Barbara Outland had qualities of reliability and integrity that meant a great deal to Arnold at a crucial time of his life. Within a short time of meeting Arnold in July 1969, she introduced him to her parents' home life, which seems to have been lived out in perfect harmony, a state that Arnold must have compared to Gustav and Aurelia's relationship with inevitable results. Barbara also provided something of an escape for Arnold, an escape from himself and the pressures of his struggle, for she, rare soul, had never heard of Arnold Schwarzenegger.

Arnold must have felt, perhaps for the first time in his life, that he was loved for himself alone. The fact that Barbara intended to teach English was an added advantage, and Arnold benefited from her guidance, patience and inspiration. Whatever the attractions, it is obvious that Arnold's feelings for Barbara were very real, probably the deepest he had felt for another person outside the confines of family life. For the first time a little of Arnold's life was no longer his own.

But the pressures of body-building continued, and acclamation increased. On the cover of the May 1969 *Muscle Builder* Arnold was trumpeted as the 'New Muscular Phenomenon', which was no less than the truth, but there were still important figures in the body-building world that Arnold needed to beat. One such was the Cuban Sergio Oliva, who was absent from the line-up of contestants for the IFBB Mr Universe competition in New York. The absence irked Arnold, who wanted Oliva there so he could vanquish him. After winning the Mr Universe, Arnold's obsession with Oliva had grown so pronounced that when he discovered his missing opponent was competing in a Mr Olympia contest that same night he persuaded the judges to let him enter as a last-minute contestant. It meant another loss for Arnold and another valuable lesson in losing, for Oliva swept the board with what Arnold realized was a thoroughly justified victory.

Oliva, and the need to make him the loser, began to take Arnold over, and his training and determination hardened towards that goal. When Arnold showed up in London to take his second Mr Universe title of the year, he was gratified, but acutely aware that, once again, the elusive Oliva was not there to compete against him. This was too much for Arnold, who now asked Joe Weider's help in building up his potential for another year in America to make him ready to crush Oliva in competition. Part of the deal seems to have been that Joe would bring over Franco Columbu to share Arnold's American dream, for Franco was a friend who had long been part of Arnold's world and understood his personality.

Moving into Arnold's small apartment, Franco consolidated his place as Arnold's closest soulmate, though Barbara was perhaps a strong opponent. When Barbara was not around, Arnold and Franco wasted no time in enjoying sexual adventures with a string of women as a relief from their strenuous training sessions. Eventually, the two men moved into a two-bedroom apartment in Santa Monica's 14th Street, and set up together as rather unlikely bricklayers, calling themselves 'Pumping Bricks'.

Some doubt seems to exist as to whether this much talked about self-employment was merely a myth; if it was not, they were certainly the world's most physically striking bricklayers. Using money acquired from their business activities, Franco and Arnold bought land, sometimes making a profit and sometimes getting their fingers burned. No catastrophe was a total loss to Arnold, who learned from every mistake just as he had in body-building. Intent on improving his mind and arming himself with the knowledge and social tools he would need to climb in America, Arnold enrolled at evening school, a move that must have deeply impressed Barbara. He was also about to become a movie star – of sorts.

How appropriate that Arnold's film debut should be in a movie about Hercules, in which —could there be any question? —he played the eponymous hero. His contract for *Hercules Goes Bananas* (later reissued to make it sound like a more serious work as *Hercules in New York* and *Hercules — The Movie*), was arranged by Joe Weider, who went straight to the heart of the movie's producers by assuring them that the newly imported Arnold Strong (as Arnold called himself at this time) had considerable experience in Shakespearean drama back home in Germany; the body they could see for themselves. According to Arnold, 'I didn't understand most of what I was saying. I stepped off the boat and starred in a motion picture. It was crazy.'

Crazy it may have been, but it was also a beginning, an ambition initiated and reasonably easily attained. If this was typical of American film-making, it did not matter that he had the most rudimentary understanding of what acting was all about. In truth it was his body the producers were after. 'See him topple two-ton newspaper rolls!' shouted the posters; 'See him toss tough men like toothpicks!'

Against Arnold's meatloaf contribution a little-known character actor, who had made his most distinguished appearance in Otto Preminger's *The Man with the Golden Arm* (1955), was cast as Arnold's co-star, though Arnold Stang, giving a faintly bemused performance as the puny, chinless pretzel-seller whom Hercules befriends, hardly seemed a likely figure to set the cinema tills ringing. There is also something a little perverse about having a movie whose two stars are called Arnold Strong and Arnold Stang — as Danny Peary said, 'That's the type of duo that would appear in *Mad Magazine* movie-poster parodies.'

Any story about Hercules cannot help but have charming possibilities, and it is some sort of achievement that the producers of this piece seem to have overlooked almost all of them. On Mount Olympus, unsmiling Zeus is unhappy about his son Hercules taking one of his do-gooding trips down to earth. 'If I'd known how much trouble it would cause me, I'd have thought twice when I met his mother on my vacation,' complains Zeus. Hercules flies to earth anyway, strikes up a sort of relationship with Pretzy (Stang), clobbers all comers who try to outdo his god-like physical prowess, and eventually outwits a gang of seedy crooks by staging an impromptu chariot race through Times Square. Most of the action and dialogue is weak, with only a glance at characterization, but where the film scores most heavily is in allowing Arnold to show off his physique, stripped down to a fetching, skimpy little Grecian costume for the Mount Olympus scenes, or stripped down to a pair of jeans in New York City. He also spends some time in a woolly hat.

Nobody working on the movie seems to have thought the public was ready to hear Arnold's voice, but his lines are expertly dubbed by a suitably dark brown voice. As an actor, though hardly startling, Arnold does not seem without resource, and is certainly already the equal of a Reg Park or Steve Reeves. Looking superb, standing and moving with an easy grace that owes much to his body-building expertise, he clearly impresses the various starlets who stand around, chests pouting, on the edges of the movie. One of these actresses, playing Hercules' earthly girlfriend, has a nasty moment in one of their scenes together when she makes a fearful hash of her lines and dries up in mid-sentence. Arnold, showing surprising maturity, exhibits a natural ability to carry on the conversation so that the cameras can keep rolling.

However diminished Arnold's achievements in body-building may have been by his eventual success in movies, 1970 was the year in which he reached his first pinnacle of supremacy. In his own words: 'I had cleaned house. That was it. It's what I call the golden triangle. I went boom, boom, boom in three cities in two weeks. I beat everybody, every formidable contender who ever existed in body-building. I was King Kong.'

Barbara was around to see the victories that the year would bring, and to help her boyfriend achieve them, stepping aside when Arnold spent long hours in rigorous training, now turning to a split and double split method of breaking down his sessions, a system inspired by Joe Weider. The year began with a devastating success scored against a man who must have winced at the irony of his own defeat — Reg Park. Park had been coaxed to re-enter the field, from which he had retired, by Wag Bennett, and had spent a year getting back into shape.

Any doubts Arnold might have had about competing with his

lifelong idol and good friend evaporated when he told himself it would be 'good for my ego and good for publicity'. When the pair met for the NABBA Mr Universe contest in London on 18 September 1970, each must have feared the possible victory of the other. A telling photograph exists in which Park and Arnold stand together during the contest, Park casting a surreptitious and anxious look at Arnold's glistening body. It is the look of a man who realizes he has made a big mistake. Some reports claim that Arnold played his not unusual trick of unnerving Park just before his entrance, drawing Park's irritation and anger. Whatever the truth, the judges proclaimed Arnold the winner.

His ambition was proving tireless. Jim Lorimer, the organizer of the Mr World competition to be held in Columbus, Ohio, on the very next day, persuaded Arnold that he should jump into a (specially commissioned) plane and play for the title. The thought does not seem to have entered Arnold's head before, but he readily agreed, no doubt influenced by the fact that the dreaded Sergio Oliva – the target he had long set himself – was also competing.

Appearing at the contest looking remarkably fresh and brilliantly sharp, Arnold walked away with the title, submitting Oliva to the degradation of second place, followed up by one-time movie hopeful Dave Draper. Arnold's joy at winning was tempered by the fact that he thought Oliva a graceless loser, but perhaps Oliva's sense of impotence against the all-powerful march of Arnold's progress is understandable.

More positively, Arnold was impressed by Jim Lorimer's enterprise and expertise, recognizing him as the sort of man he wanted around him in his career, though he knew the moment had not yet come for him to be able to maximize Lorimer's potential. Lorimer responded equally positively when Arnold told him he would come back to see him in the future and make him his partner, a promise Arnold was to keep, to the advantage of both men.

Any doubts Oliva had about his abdication of body-building's crown to Arnold were ended when Arnold again beat him at New York Town Hall at the IFBB Mr Olympia competition; Arnold's 'boom, boom, boom' was complete. So far as body-building was concerned, he had nowhere to go but down, nowhere to stay but level. And anyone who knew Arnold at all well by now realized that Arnold was interested only in going up.

Looking at *Hercules Goes Bananas*, Arnold must have felt that acting classes might help him, and he took them. Steve Reeves, Reg Park and the bulging catalogue of screen musclemen had shown the way, and hadn't Arnold already proved himself the physical equal of any of them? As he waited for his acting career to become real (and he would not have long to wait) he turned to exploiting his other skills, his business talents encouraged by the dealings of Joe Weider.

A new generation of men, who had once responded to the promises of Charles Atlas that never again would a strong he-man kick sand in their face, sent off for body-building courses and products marketed by Arnold under his blatantly self-explanatory pseudonym of Arnold Strong. Body-building courses supposedly written by Mr Strong (but in reality the work of Weider's right-hand man and editor) spread Arnold's fame and brought in a great deal of money. Barbara's support extended to office duties, as Arnold endeavoured to become, every day, that little bit better known. His progress, which by the end of 1970 might have settled down into a contented steady enjoyment of his body-building successes, was in fact about to surge forward.

After all, Arnold had always known there were better things to life than Austria and a humdrum life. Success, and acclaim, in whatever way it could be gained. However it could be got. Body-building – or movies.

4   Movie Muscle

If 1970 was Arnold's year of triumph, 1971 was the year when he was pulled back to his Austrian roots with the death of Meinhard. Arnold was now living with Barbara, and his life had proved altogether more spectacular and favoured than that of his elder brother, who had once been the darling of his parents. As Arnold's career blossomed, Meinhard had to stand by and watch his own life stretching out flatly before him. The brightest hope in Meinhard's life was the fact that he had fallen in love with a woman who was kind and genuinely fond of him, and had given him a son.

Unfortunately, Meinhard's insecurity led to bouts of drinking and – much to Gustav's chagrin – trouble with the law. Sentenced to a prison sentence after assaulting an old lady, Meinhard walked free determined to do better for himself and his family, but it was not to be. In late May, 1971, Meinhard took his car out after a heavy drinking session, crashed it, and was killed. It emerged later that, throughout the difficult times when Meinhard had been unable to support Erika and their son Patrick adequately, Arnold had supplied moral and financial support, a support that continued after Meinhard's death. Perhaps feeling that nothing would be served by it, Arnold did not attend the funeral.

That summer Arnold travelled to Paris to take the Mr Olympia title, but his reputation and continuing physical supremacy made this seem almost a foregone conclusion. He defended and retained the title for the next four years, to return again to be named Mr Olympia in 1980.

Aurelia's sorrow at the death of her eldest son was compounded by the death of Gustav in December 1972 at the age of sixty-five, but her surviving son did not travel to Austria for the funeral. Arnold painted an unflattering portrait of his reasons for not doing so in a film he would shortly make but, whatever the true reasons may have been, his absence did not do irreparable damage to his relationship with Aurelia. As so many photographs of the two testify, she is the battered willow clinging to the mighty oak for support and protection from the world, a support and protection that Arnold is always ready to supply.

Meanwhile, Arnold continued to attract people who would prove to be crucially important in his future career. It was in the autumn of 1972 that he was approached by the photographer George Butler, sent to the Mr America competition in Brooklyn as part of his research for a new book he was planning with author Charles Gaines, which they had thought of calling *Pumping Iron*.

Seeing Arnold, Butler, like so many before him, was impressed. Not only did Arnold have the body, but he had the ego, the personality, the charisma, that made him the outstanding body-builder of his time, and the one that Butler immediately realized would provide the core and *raison d'être* both for the book — and the film of the book — that he and Gaines were working on. Once again important figures were investing in Arnold. Meanwhile, his career as an actor moved slowly ahead.

In 1973, Arnold managed a walk-on role for Robert Altman's well-received Raymond Chandler mystery *The Long Goodbye*, starring Elliott Gould, though he still insisted on being billed as Arnold Strong. A friend, David Arkin, had suggested Arnold to Altman, who saw him and was impressed enough to give him a little screentime as a heavy towards the end of the movie. Though hardly a breakthrough, it did represent his first appearance in a mainstream film, with a director and actors whom the public had heard of and might pay to see, unlike poor *Hercules Goes Bananas*. Arnold was now keeping better company.

Some allies in his progress to the top seemed a little unlikely. Arnold's personal appearances on chat shows were many and skilfully managed, with Arnold drawing attention to the joys of body-building by equating it to good sex. Lucille Ball happened to be watching

The Merv Griffin Show on TV when Arnold was one of the guests, and liked what she saw. Soon Arnold found himself in a TV special with Art Carney, produced by the indefatigable Miss Ball, who cast him as a masseur. She went to the trouble of paying for some acting lessons to help him prepare for the role, thus adding her distinguished name to the growing supporters of the up-and-coming young actor.

The role Charles Gaines played in Arnold's life took on a new importance in 1974, and not only because the book of *Pumping Iron* was published (after considerable resistance from publishers who thought its generous photographic offering of rippling manhood was simply an excuse to titillate 'fags'). The book brought the film version closer, and interested director Bob Rafelson in the whole business of body-building, leading him to Gaines' earlier novel *Stay Hungry*, which Rafelson now decided to turn into a movie. It was Gaines who suggested to Rafelson that Arnold might be the ideal person to fill the role of Joe Santo, a likeable, characterful body-builder who is the pivot of the book's events. At first dubious, Rafelson met Arnold, realized his potential, and offered him the part.

'Bob Rafelson . . . was the first one to send me to acting school before I did *Stay Hungry*. He sent me to all the various television shows and movies that were made in town so that I could watch and get used to the dialogue, and to what "cut", "action", "speed", and all that means . . . so I really started educating myself and put the same kind of energy into it as I did with body-building.'

Being third-billed to Jeff Bridges and Sally Field in a movie to be directed by the man who had helped make Jack Nicholson's name with two brilliant works, *Five Easy Pieces* (1970) and *The King of Marvin Gardens* (1972), looked like progress, and showed how clearly Arnold's plan of transmuting from body-builder into film actor was coming alive. But a price for his ambition had to be paid.

Barbara, who had long supported Arnold in his ascent to the throne of body-building, was now a qualified English teacher in Los Angeles. Perhaps she felt she had done enough, and that once this ambition had been answered Arnold would settle into a steadier lifestyle. The signing of the *Stay Hungry* contract showed her that this was not so, and when he left home to begin the shoot in April 1975 Barbara decided to walk out of Arnold's life.

Turning to *Stay Hungry*, Arnold had to satisfy Rafelson's demands that he should tone down his body for the role (really a question of losing a little weight), and learn something about acting. He enrolled with a coach, Eric Morris, with whom he studied for twelve weeks, towards the end of which period he began work on the movie. Accent removal classes became an important part of the regime. Very soon Arnold, with his quick intelligence, began learning things about the craft he was now embarking on that Eric Morris, or any other drama coach, could never have taught him. He came to enjoy hanging out with actors, listening to their conversations, finding what made them function, coming to an understanding of the special mentality that makes an actor. Standing beside Jeff Bridges, Arnold came to appreciate how Bridges could steal a scene from him with the merest inflection or glance or movement. Perhaps fortified by the techniques he had perfected to unnerve other body-builders in competition, Arnold began to find ways of deflecting attention away from the other actors he appeared with. Luckily he got on well with Bridges, whom he respected as a professional.

As for Rafelson, he quickly agreed that Gaines' suggestion had been highly satisfactory, that Arnold was the right man – or, now, the right actor – for the role. Gaines was interested to discover how like the character he was playing in the movie Arnold actually was; he had an eerie feeling that the fictional character had somehow been based on Arnold. When filming wound up, Rafelson told Arnold he looked forward to making more movies with him, a hope that has not yet materialized.

Louis Pitt, Arnold's agent at this time, summed up Arnold's achievement, and the resistance he had met with in getting so far into the industry: 'I think that there was scepticism on other people's part only because nobody had really succeeded in that area . . . Looking at *Stay Hungry*, you could see that there was more to the person than body-building, even though it was centred around that idea. Arnold wanted to be exploited, take that attention, take that notoriety, use that to beget other things. So it became a kind of systematic plot plan.'

In fact, Arnold couldn't have landed in a happier movie at this stage of his career, for *Stay Hungry* is quirky, likeable when it's not being lovable, and gives a delightful overview of its characters and situations – it is one of the most intelligent movies Arnold has ever made, and definitely has a higher quota of charm than most others in his canon.

Its story centres on the well-to-do but restless Alabama hero Craig Blake (Bridges) who gets inside a gymnasium to persuade its owner to sell and clear the way for lucrative land development. Once inside, Blake is fascinated by the body-builders who work out there, including Joe Santo (Arnold), apparently a one-time Mr Austria. Helping Blake to a new appreciation of life, Joe introduces Blake to the type of girl he would otherwise have been unlikely to meet, the decidedly downtown Mary Tate (Sally Field).

Along the way Arnold flexes up dressed in a rubber 'Batman' costume, and does an excellent impression of playing the fiddle when Joe is discovered playing in a blue-grass band. A set-piece highlight is the Mr Universe title, in which the contestants, like huge chorines, gradually make their appearance coming up on a revolving stage.

Not perhaps as successfully integrated as it might have been, *Stay Hungry* was nevertheless a distinguished and probing film, and one that had a real interest in its people. When the movie premiered, after a long delay, in June 1976, Arnold came in for a great deal of attention and a good deal of praise at the Hollywood Golden Globe Awards for 1977, and was awarded Best Male Acting Debut for his role in the movie. The evening was only soured by the fact that the spotlight kept falling on an actor called Sylvester Stallone, whose breakthrough movie, *Rocky*, was named Motion Picture of the Year. In the world of movies, as in the world of body-building, Arnold was going to have to cope with opponents, and, being Arnold, there was only one thing to be done – beat them at their own game. It was clear that Stallone represented a very real threat to his supremacy.

Arnold came from the world of body-building, and knew its history. As he said: 'Most Americans didn't know what body-building was. There was only a small group of people doing it on Muscle Beach. I took it away from the days of 500 liver pills and 2,000 sit-ups and eight hours sleep a night and made it more casual. I felt we had to educate people about it.'

If *Pumping Iron* had been the only film by which Arnold is remembered, it would itself have earned him a claim to significant cult status. Now, in the context of his subsequent career, we have this extraordinary document, a reminder of his kingship of body-building, apparently betraying many aspects of his character (some of which he later tried to explain away) and at the same time suggesting that he had a natural talent for his own kind of acting.

In 1985, Arnold put forward the view that *Pumping Iron* was 'all designed, very thoroughly, to sell the idea of body-building . . . Sex is something everybody understands, so I compared body-building with sex. In the mid-seventies, my job was to sell body-building to the general public. And I did.'

The great move forward would not have happened without George Butler, the man who had met Arnold in September 1972 and been so taken with him that he made Arnold the central attraction of his project. Butler conceived the idea of building a documentary film about the world of body-building, based on his 1974 book, which would in effect be a vehicle for Arnold, the other body-builders unconsciously making up a very supporting cast.

Arnold was buoyed up when Butler told him that he would not consider making the movie without him, and a deal was struck, despite the fact that Arnold's ambitions were already turning away from the sport that had made his name. By 1974 Arnold said he was 'sick and tired of it. But it happened slowly. So I said to myself, "If that isn't there, get out." But I couldn't, because I didn't have a replacement for it.' *Pumping Iron*, by the strangest of ironies about the very occupation that he had wearied of, was the perfect opportunity to head off in a new direction.

By the time filming began in June 1975 Arnold also had more confidence as an actor, having worked hard to pick up some of the craft needed for his burgeoning screen career. The technique used to present Arnold on-screen in *Pumping Iron* makes considerable use of these skills, for Arnold is not only required to be his own awesome physical self, but is seen living out his everyday life, either speaking directly to an off-screen interviewer or interacting with fellow body-builders and associates. According to those who made the film, the piece was not actually scripted, but Arnold's claim that the documentary was 'all designed' suggests the director's hand in shaping the content of Arnold's conversational sequences. If Arnold, at the outset and during the making of the movie, was content to present what appeared to be a true self-portrait on screen, he later denied this was what he handed in.

For the set-piece gladiatorial climax of *Pumping Iron* Butler and Arnold decided on the finals of the Mr Olympia contest held in Pretoria, South Africa, on 8 November 1975, in which Arnold would be attempting to take his sixth consecutive title. Even as he trained mercilessly to achieve such an extraordinary goal, Arnold was aware that he was about to leave the world of professional competition body-building to conquer new domains, and told Butler as much during the making of the movie. He was also already, and wisely, investing the money he was beginning to accumulate in buying up real estate, presiding over a burgeoning business empire built up through his own tenacity and hard work. By the time *Pumping Iron* was showing in America, Arnold owned four substantial buildings in Los Angeles, had his own lucrative mail-order company and managed his own lecture tours, building on his hard-won reputation as the world's greatest body-builder. He was also buying up a coal mine in West Virginia.

When shooting on *Pumping Iron* wound up, Butler conceived an immense, arty stunt that Barnum would surely have been proud of. Recognizing in Arnold's overweening ambition 'a mixture of Nietzschean philosophy and a Soviet five-year-plan', Butler responded with a ruse calculated to further Arnold's fame and build interest in the forthcoming movie. He persuaded the curators of the Whitney Museum in New York to let him present, for one night only (giving the event another true feel of the travelling show), a display of *tableaux vivants* in which, close to sculptures by Rodin and Michelangelo, Arnold (this time with a supporting cast of only two, Frank Zane and Ed Corney) would pose, turn, flex and exhibit. The title given to the event suggests its intellectual appeal: 'Articulate Muscle: The Body as Art.'

When the evening of the exhibition arrived, 25 February 1976, some 3,000 paying customers filed into the Museum to gaze at the three presentations of living male beauty. The event was as important to Arnold as it was to the world of body-building or the sensation-seeking punters. For some, the exaggerated sculptures presented by the trio of Titans on display might revive memories of physiques handed down in legend by such as the Great Sandow, reminding nineteenth century audiences of the potential splendours of the male body. Others saw this official sanctioning of the physical art as a vindication of body-building, at one stroke sweeping away the sordid and dubious aura that had so long hung around this activity.

Arnold's achievement helped to transmute body-building into something that now reclaimed its substantial classical credentials. His body reminded those that came to gaze on it that the roots for his lust for physical perfection were to be found in antiquity. By a supreme effort, Arnold and his supporters were making positive, god-like, beautiful efforts to revive those superhuman, desirable, manly wonders that had been lost or forgotten.

With one brilliant stroke Arnold had placed himself at the centre of a happening that focused all attention on his prime asset, before a new and different audience, in a context that would help him along the way to becoming seen as a serious artist in a misunderstood medium. The accumulated furniture of all his years as a body-builder was, quite subtly, being discarded at the very moment when he seemed to be exploiting it to the fullest.

'There's not a top body-builder without a good mind,' said Arnold around this time. 'If a writer produces a book, nobody says "My God, that means he has a puny body." A body-builder isn't out to prove his intellect at the moment he is performing.'

Pumping Iron was eventually released in New York on 18 January 1977, when Arnold's contribution was lauded by many critics. Richard Schickel in *Time* saw his potential as 'a multimedia presence of some force . . . A cool, shrewd and boyish charmer, he exudes the easy confidence of a man who has always known he will be a star of some kind.' *New York* magazine announced that 'Schwarzenegger lights up the film like neon every time he comes on stage . . . he looks like a walking incarnation of the Mighty Thor.'

Such praise, of course, had to be built on. Arnold was at the head of the *Pumping Iron* publicity machine, but was helped along the road of fame by many – sometimes surprising – new friends. Andy Warhol was pleased to make his acquaintance, Jacqueline Kennedy's company invested Arnold with a touch of class, and no less a headline-getting photographer than Robert Mapplethorpe wanted to snap him, immortalize that body, encapsulate that charisma. The *Pumping Iron* roller-coaster reached its peak when Arnold went to the Cannes Film Festival in July 1977 to publicize the movie. Fifty thousand people crowded the beach to see him cavort with a gaggle of pretty girls for a photograph session.

Butler's movie has a huge potency, wrapped up in a piece that may look artless but is cunningly put together and brilliant in its composition and exposition. The first shock of the film is to see Arnold and Franco Columbu taking a ballet class at the barre, assuming some of the athletic, gazelle-like grace of the dancer. We notice at once that Arnold has a strong desire to learn from those who can teach him something that will be useful to him, a willingness to absorb the best instruction that can be offered.

When Arnold, five-times winner of the Mr Olympia contest, arrives to train for his next competition at Gold's Gym in Venice, California, he is given a hero's welcome. He tells his mates he has already telephoned his mother to tell her he has won the title for the sixth time. We see Arnold making a personal appearance at a federal prison, and appreciate the skill with which he controls the crowd of inmates gathered around him in admiration. One of the men offers to kiss him, provoking a beautifully timed response from Arnold, a slow burn of amusement followed by the invitation to 'Come over here and I'll give you a kiss.' Everybody laughs, and Arnold strips off to reveal his torso. Amusement is turned to wonder. Arnold is in charge.

In his straight-to-camera moments Arnold further displays an assurance that sits on him with incredible ease. At some length he likens body-building to sex, explains that it is as if he is 'coming' all day long, is all day in Heaven. Such sexual ecstasy can only be heightened by the confession that, from the age of ten, he has idolized legendary people, including dictators and Jesus – anyone who has a capacity to be remembered for thousands of years. It is rumoured that Arnold also declared an admiration for Hitler before the cameras, but no trace of this is left in the completed movie, and Arnold has subsequently refuted this suggestion.

Anyone unimpressed by Arnold's physique will surely be won over by his supreme self-absorption. The most telling manifestation of this is the account he gives in the movie of his reaction to Gustav's death. If we are to believe his on-screen explanation, his mother telephoned him with news of her husband's death, and naturally expected that Arnold would return to Austria for the funeral. Arnold declined, pointing out that he was preparing for a championship contest and could not be diverted from his preparation at so crucial a stage.

Arnold later said this scene was a complete fabrication put in at the request of others, introduced to give colour and bite to his character; it certainly showed a degree of ruthlessness. According to him, Aurelia was 'pissed off' when she saw this sequence. Arnold's explanation seems to be a peculiarly contrary story for him to have told simply to please the film-makers. Watching the film, we believe this is really Arnold talking about his own life, playing himself.

The first experience we have of an actual contest is in the section of the movie dealing with the amateur Mr Universe title, finally battled out between assured Ken Waller and nervous Mike Katz. They would be mincemeat if they were pitted against Arnold. That privilege is reserved for Louis (Lou) Ferrigno (who was eventually to find some sort of success as TV's *Incredible Hulk*) and pint-sized superman Franco Columbu.

Columbu, long-standing friend, partner and rival, is shown as a perfectly formed acorn to Arnold's oak. Butler gives us a wholly sympathetic picture of Columbu, and we can only warm to him as

he sits unassumingly with his very Italian family, sharing their simple life. Unfortunately, Columbu is reduced to a sort of stunt-man
by what we see of him, lifting a car out of a tight parking-space and
blowing up hot-water bottles until they explode in his face. We
would be hard-pressed to imagine Arnold resorting to such fair-
ground tactics.

The depiction of Lou Ferrigno is even more touching. A Mr
America and (twice) Mr Universe, 24-year-old Ferrigno, an ex-
sheet-metalworker from Brooklyn, stands at 6'5" and weighs in at
275 pounds – the biggest body-builder of all time. Handicapped
from childhood by a hearing disability, Ferrigno's entire world re-
volves around body-building and the love of muscle, a love
nurtured by his father Matty, who has retired from the police force
to train his pliable son. Ferrigno has only one true idol in his world
– Arnold, the man he now wants to oust from power. Louis' father
likens Arnold to God, and knows Arnold is a dangerous beast, ruthless in competition. Matty's adoration of Lou and Lou's love for
Matty is both striking and sad.

While Columbu and Ferrigno are shown to us surrounded by
their admiring families and loved ones, Arnold stands alone, unen-
cumbered by familial comfort, but able (as is clear at the end of the
movie) to at any time make himself a part of Ferrigno's close-knit
family circle. Always friendly to Ferrigno and Columbu, there is
nonetheless no question as to who is in charge of the relationships.
It is Arnold's natural role. Though Arnold has an obvious fondness
for Columbu and Ferrigno, he assures us that such sentiment will
not be allowed to get in the way of his winning the prize. He lays out
his technique for us. The undermining of Ferrigno's confidence by
Arnold is cunning, and goes apparently undetected by the ingenuous Ferrigno. Arnold is sure he can mess Ferrigno up the night
before the contest, effectively talking him into losing. Arnold's attitude to Columbu, as the day of the contest arrives, is similarly
robust: 'Franco is a child,' Arnold explains. 'When it comes to the
day of the contest I'm his father.'

Mike Spitz is said to have told Arnold that a favourite trick of his
own was to make a very obvious point of checking that everything
was as it should be in his swimming trunks at the very second when

the competitors' concentration should be on their performance. Unnerved by Spitz's action, the competitors' attention switches at the crucial moment to their crotches.

As for Arnold, his tactic has obviously not changed since he told Charles Gaines during the writing of the original *Pumping Iron* book that 'I can be very friendly off-stage, but on-stage I will pull one trick after another on my competitor to wipe him out, you know because it's my living and I have to win. Franco is my best friend, but I will do as much as I can to make him look bad and make me look good.'

Looking good he may have been, though there were always those on hand to see the slightly comical side of his achievements. To Clive James, Arnold resembled 'a condom stuffed with walnuts'.

Louise Sweet in the *Monthly Film Bulletin* discovered that 'the fusion of mind and body in Schwarzenegger is what surprises the viewer,' not least because 'the art of body-building, after all, as the film makes clear, is not for the man who has everything, but for those who can do nothing else'. Sweet's glowing account of Arnold's performance was perceptive; she found his articulateness and humour made the movie cohere and convince, and explained that 'the grandness (even grossness) of Schwarzenegger's aspirations become acceptable, even attractive, because they are dealt with humorously and because in our uncertain quest to buy perfection we cannot help admiring someone who attains a classical ideal'.

Arnold's prison scene in *Pumping Iron* gives some idea of the work he has consistently done in US prisons since that time, often taking monthly seminars, the popularity of which is hardly surprising. It was the sort of work, too, that looks forward to the missionary role Arnold would be given by George Bush many years later with the creation of the National Health and Fitness Council. When it came to prisons, 'The impact there is much more psychological. Building their bodies and getting strong was really the first time they'd done something positive for themselves. And when they were released they felt right away a sense of belonging when they went into a gym outside. That's better than being dropped off at some bus station with $20 in their pocket and back on the street committing crimes.'

More modest work followed, as Arnold waited for the next giant move ahead. In 1976 he played in an episode of *The Streets of San Francisco* with its regular star Karl Malden, but Arnold knew his aspirations did not end in a television studio. At this time, there was also some talk of his being picked for the *Superman* extravaganza, but though its producers sent for clippings of Arnold in *Stay Hungry* and *Pumping Iron* they eventually decided against hiring him. By the end of 1976 Arnold himself was not too keen on the idea, saying he could not make his mind up about the picture until he had read Mario Puzo's script. And, if he should land the role, 'it could go either way – very good or not so good – bad. I think if I would do *Superman* now that's what I would be known as – just a Superman'.

It was pretty clear that Arnold was already displaying the ability to have as positive thoughts about the movie business as about body-building. How else could it be, now that he had decided to conquer it?

5   A Sort of Male Jayne Mansfield

Anyone wanting an account of Arnold's life can do no better than read the book he wrote in the mid-seventies, *Arnold: The Education of a Body-builder*, co-written with Douglas Kent Hall, which turns out to be half autobiography and half instruction manual for would-be body-builders.

Disarmingly, Arnold appears to write briefly but with a sort of brutal honesty about his upbringing and early years. Immodesty does not figure largely here, but there is much of interest. As to any close relationships with women, the book was only in time to catch his friendship with Barbara Outland, which was replaced during the seventies by his relationships first with Sue Moray and subsequently – and it appears simultaneously – with Maria Shriver.

Sue Moray came upon Arnold as the all-healthy, blonde-haired, sparky-tongued American girl, sailing into his vision on roller skates at Venice Beach. Twenty-five years old, pretty and personable, she worked as an assistant at a Vidal Sassoon salon in Beverly Hills, though Arnold, ever ready to use his influence, soon found her a similar appointment at a salon near Gold's Gym, so that he and Sue should not be far apart. The physicality of the relationship was always important, and before very long Sue moved into Arnold's apartment, where they enjoyed a full and satisfying relationship. Arnold persuaded her that it should be 'open'; when away from home their closeness should not prevent either of them from finding satisfaction elsewhere.

Under what circumstances the friendship might have flourished we cannot tell, for Arnold's life took another turn in late August 1977 when he attended the Robert F. Kennedy Tennis Tournament

at Forest Hills and met Maria Shriver, Joe Kennedy's granddaugh-
ter and the daughter of Eunice K. Shriver and Sargent Shriver.
Maria's qualifications were more all-American than Sue Moray's,
and with her strong Kennedy background she must have seemed of
irresistible interest to Arnold. Suddenly a friendship with one of
America's greatest and most legendary families was opening up before him, yet another sign that Arnold's Midas touch was holding
out.

Born on 6 November 1955, Maria had lived in Paris for a time
when her father became Ambassador there, and had later spent a
short and unhappy period at a kibbutz in Israel. In 1972 Sargent
Shriver ran for Vice-President in the US elections, travelling over
America accompanied by Maria, who was surrounded by the press
corps that attached itself to the campaign. Both her parents had
worked in the media at one time or another, and Maria was attracted to such a life. When Arnold and she met, Maria had just
graduated from university after majoring in American Studies.

The meeting at Forest Hills was successful enough for them to
want to meet again, and it was she who invited him to weekend at
Hyannis Port and there meet the Kennedy family. Arnold was later
to say that for Maria it was love at first sight, but his regard for her
followed a slower path. Things were smoothed by the fact that the
Kennedys welcomed him warmly (after all, he was a success story
amongst a family whose own successes had suffered some devastating reverses), and they must have been aware that he had always
admired the Kennedys, even if he had never been particularly
enthusiastic about their politics. In 1985 Arnold said of his
relationship with Maria, 'It makes me respect a girl much more if
she's independent. It makes me respect Maria tremendously because she's very bright, because she's a go-getter, because she's very
hungry for knowledge all the time . . . She has different beliefs, a
different upbringing from me. She grew up in a different culture,
had a different educational background, a different political background. All of this just makes it ideal.'

The difficulty for Arnold was that the relationships with Sue and
Maria (conducted thousands of miles apart) had to be resolved – a
choice had to be made. Sue became aware of her lover's friendship

with the Kennedy heiress, but seems to have put up with it and some unsympathetic treatment from Arnold until August 1978, when she moved out of Arnold's apartment, if not completely out of his life. The couple still saw each other occasionally, but it was clear to Sue that Arnold had determined that his real future lay with Maria.

Relationships at this stage of Arnold's career – and later, too – tended to come second to professional commitments. *Stay Hungry* and *Pumping Iron* had been highly satisfactory beginnings, but had to be followed up. Towards the end of the seventies, the best that seemed to be on offer was a spoof western that promised to make funny men out of its two male leads. A misplaced sense of humour may help to explain what went wrong with this welcome prospect.

When *The Villain* left the US to play in other countries, its title was changed to *Cactus Jack*, which may partly have been because of a wish that the distributors wanted to distance themselves from the critical panning the movie had received on its American showing. On the face of it this should have been another important lucky break for Arnold, third-billed below no less than Kirk Douglas – one of the very few Hollywood superstars Arnold has worked with – and Ann-Margret.

The fact that the script looked none too promising did not prevent Arnold from signing up, but only a desperate need to be in any film anywhere can explain Douglas' involvement in this sorry affair, a comedy that stubbornly refused to be in the least amusing. When shooting began in Tucson, Arizona, in October 1978, it may have seemed possible to make something genuinely entertaining of *The Villain*, but this must soon have dissolved into a far-off hope.

The fault probably lies principally with its director Hal Needham, a Tennessee-born stuntman who graduated to making movies instead of merely arranging their pratfalls. It is no surprise that Needham's films, especially those in which he established a profitable working relationship with Burt Reynolds, had their generous helpings of action, sometimes, as in the 1977 *Smokey and the Bandit*, resulting in a decent, successful piece of work. In *The Villain* Needham's theme is the adventures of a Wild West baddy (constantly checking what he should be doing in a villain's textbook) whose every dastardly ploy collapses around him, leaving him time and again hoist on his own petard.

It was up to the luckless Robert G. Kane to concoct a screenplay around this idea in a story that was done within a few minutes and then dragged along into nothingness. Luscious Charming Jones (Ann-Margret) is charged with conveying the fortunes of her father's mining discoveries, assisted by the naïve, unexpectedly gentlemanly and well-proportioned Handsome Stranger (Arnold). An untrustworthy Bank Manager (Jack Elam) intends to wrest the fortune from Charming, and despatch Handsome. Cactus Jack (Douglas), an incompetent but resilient villain, whose only under-standing ally is his horse Whisky, is waiting to be hanged when the Bank Manager gets him out of prison on the understanding that he will do his dirty work for him.

Arnold, compressed into a Lone Ranger outfit, looks stunning, is not required to bare so much as a single pectoral, and shows that he has made no very significant advance in his acting despite his taking the $275,000 fee. The gags he is involved in fall no flatter than any others in the movie, including helping old ladies across streets they do not wish to cross, bravely stopping a team of runaway horses that happen to be taking the fire engine to a blaze at the local whore-house, and displaying a wide range of sexual innocence.

Ann-Margret, dangerously near to spilling out of Bob Mackie's genuinely funny dresses, does an impression of a Barbie Doll that is frighteningly accurate, but this is a sad comedown after her recent contribution to Richard Attenborough's spooky *Magic* (1978). In her scenes with Arnold she seems unsure whether his *entendre* are supposed to be *double* or not.

The main sadness of this film is to see Douglas amiably throwing himself around the screen as he tries to eliminate his prey. The jokes are signposted for miles ahead, though the creators may have planned this as part of the piece's quirky charm. In a film that too often has a mean, pinched look, the use of no fewer than eleven stunt men also seems a little over the top. Final nails in the coffin of *The Villain* are provided by the relentless milking of the comic pos-sibilities of horses, a tedious over-use of camera trickery, and a musical score so crude as to beggar belief.

Ultimately Douglas' stature is demeaned by all this, and scuppered by the absurd and crass finale in which Charming suddenly realizes Cactus Jack's sexual appeal and walks over to his side, leaving Arnold dumbstruck and Douglas (that is, one of his eleven stunt men) to do a ridiculous speeded-up Benny Hill-like gymnastic routine over the available rooftops. Only Paul Lynde, doing a gorgeously revue-like turn as an Indian Chief with a nervous disposition, has the measure of the movie, makes us smile and helps Douglas to achieve at least one faintly diverting scene.

At its original running time of almost two hours, *The Villain* must have been truly unbearable, and even in its truncated state remains an object-lesson in how to squander the undoubted talents of its three star performers. Its reception was exceedingly poor. Paul Taylor for the *Monthly Film Bulletin* discovered that 'desperation is the keynote'. He went on: 'Given the script's model and the film's determined cataloguing of "anything goes" incongruities, it seems somewhat perverse that Douglas should not be equipped with Wile E. Coyote's celebrated armoury of Acme products, or that Schwarzenegger's passive pose is not broken for even a single "beep".'

When Arnold took Maria to the 1979 Cannes Film Festival to help promote *The Villain*, he can have had little belief that this would be the movie to see him striking out on a more positive film career. As it happened, his next foray into pictures was a tribute to a fellow-performer whose physical contributions were as vital to her fame as Arnold's physical contributions were to his.

Arnold's determination to be a fully paid-up American took a giant stride in November 1979 when he graduated from the University of Wisconsin in Superior with a general business degree in the international marketing of physical fitness, a degree that suited Arnold as it would have no other. He further proved his intelligence by turning down the opportunity to appear in a disaster called *Sextette* as an appendage to the aged Mae West.

It was now time for Arnold to get a glimpse into the world of a another equally infamous film personality – Jayne Mansfield.

There were many lessons to be learned from *The Jayne Mansfield Story*, a made-for-television attempt to distil that most pneumatic of film starlets – or stars (if she could justify the sobriquet – her residency as a leading lady in Hollywood was very temporary) into a trim biopic. Unfortunately, the script was all too reminiscent of the rough-and-ready efforts that had often scuppered Mansfield's screen career, as the bemused writers (two to write the screenplay and two others credited with 'adapting' it) dug deep to present a thoroughly shallow account of their subject. 'Oh Jayne, you're not really serious about wanting to be in pictures?' asks a fellow-pop-corn-seller at a cinema, as the splendidly single-minded star-to-be dismisses a missing husband with the explanation that 'He just doesn't understand those auditions and things . . . he doesn't be-lieve in me.'

Vera Jane Palmer, born in 1933 in Bryn Mawr, Pennsylvania, was a young woman with an IQ of 163 when she decided to take a fast ticket to fame via cheesecake and her *alter ego* Jayne Mansfield. Any symptoms of higher intelligence are missing from this movie, however, where our Jayne looks as if she might have invented the word bimbo. The performance by Loni Anderson soon subsides into a roller-coaster of wiggling bottom and tiresome *moués*, as her young daughter reassures her that 'I think you're prettier than Mar-ilyn Monroe' ('Oh baby, you're my biggest fan,' replies Mom), but there is enough here to suggest that Anderson might have handed in a good performance if her writers and director had been up to the mark. Still, there are the obstacles of Raymond Buktenica's grossly embarrassing and visibly embarrassed agent, and the terrifying sweetness of little Laura Jacoby as little Jayne Marie. And then there was Arnold as the bedrock of Mansfield's emotional life, Mickey Hargitay.

Beefcake to Mansfield's cheesecake, Hargitay becomes the spe-cial man in her life when she sees him posing in a floorshow, *The Mae West Revue*. Arnold certainly has the muscles for the still-life sequences, but it is in the acting scenes where he is stretched to the full. Anderson and he must convince us of Mansfield and Hargi-tay's very sexual and deep affection for one another, of Hargitay's tremendous support of his wife, and of the gradual disintegration of their life together as Mansfield's career slipped, dipped and flopped in a miasma of low-grade movies (some so feeble they remain undistributed to this day), drunken tantrums (a chance here for the make-up designer to add hollow cheeks and sunken eyes) and squalid 'cabaret' appearances in strip joints, singing a desperately sad 'Put Your Arms Around Me, Honey' to a bunch of disinterested sleazeballs.

As Mansfield messes up, Hargitay provides a consistent decent thread, and it is here that Arnold scores in demonstrating those qualities that make Hargitay staunch and clear-minded. This is undeniably an amateur performance, but in the context the very lack of professionalism is an advantage. At times during the movie it seems that Arnold has no talent for acting whatsoever, merely bringing along a physique like a brick wall and his pleasantly gappy smile, but there is an undercurrent of reality that seems, taking into consideration the flummery with which it is filled, the only good thing about this picture.

Arnold does not always cope with his lines too well, often sounding as if he is working through the latest *Janet and John* adventure, but even this imparts a deft charm to the proceedings. Somewhere in Arnold's vague stab at portraying Hargitay is the ability of a natural talent to project from the inside of his character, indeed, so lifelike was Arnold's impersonation during a love scene with Anderson that the actress pushed him away with the promise that if she ever got divorced she would bear him in mind. Despite Arnold's physical prowess, however, it seemed inconceivable that, within a very few years, he would be Hollywood's greatest and most powerful asset.

What the Jayne Mansfield movie had provided for Arnold was a wonderful opportunity for art to mirror life. Musing on the dangerous personality of his beloved, Hargitay explains to his audience that 'It really mattered to her, the whole business of being a success. I always wondered what it was replacing in her life. What need did it fill?'

At this stage of what was already proving a real movie career, it is tempting to think that Arnold might have turned these words back on himself, suggesting that learning about Mansfield's life pointed up difficulties that might lie ahead for a prospective film actor. Alas, Mansfield, despite her very considerable strength of purpose, endurance and resilience, had none of Arnold's sticking-power;

Bette Davis, in a typically generous remark, said of her that 'Dramatic art, in her opinion, is knowing how to fill a sweater.'

Mansfield's manipulation of her career was ultimately destructive; her end summary and dreadful. Early in the morning of 28 June 1967 a car in which she was travelling to a chat-show engagement with her then-boyfriend and children was in a head-on collision with a trailer truck. Mansfield's head was torn off. Of the passengers, the children alone survived.

Looking at this movie, it sometimes seems as if Jayne Mansfield is Arnold in female form – a point picked up by some who saw his next movie. Like him she had enormous innate intelligence and a superb physical presence which she used as an entrée to the movie business. There the comparison must end, however, for Mansfield's career was a rapid decline into the footnotes of Hollywood history. Though she started with some early promising pictures such as *The Girl Can't Help It*, and her considerable stage and screen hit *Will Success Spoil Rock Hunter?*, she then escaped to Britain for three unlikely features, including *The Sheriff of Fractured Jaw* (1958) opposite Kenneth More. After this she was sentenced to some relentless rubbish – *Primitive Love* (an Italian effort made in 1964), and the Gene Kelly-directed *A Guide for the Married Man* (1966) where she was safely tucked away among a bevy of guest artistes. If nothing else, this involvement with the life of our Jayne sounded a warning note to our Arnold about how not to conduct his career.

Despite his burgeoning film career, Arnold could still not resist the opportunity to return to body-building, once more to assert the supremacy he had always enjoyed; when it came to the 1980 Mr Olympia contest, held in Australia, Arnold's eleventh-hour decision to compete for the title was possibly influenced by the fact that his old rival and colleague Frank Zane looked ripe for the trophy. Though he trained for only eight weeks, it was almost inevitable that Arnold would win, a feat recorded in a made-for-video documentary of the event, *The Comeback*.

6   Barbaric Success

After the duds that *The Villain* and *The Jayne Mansfield Story* had undoubtedly been, it was time for an upturn in Arnold's film fortunes. In fact a project had been waiting in the wings, for in many ways *Conan the Barbarian* had been hanging around waiting for Arnold since the early 1930s. The invention of the writer Robert E. Howard, this elemental protégé of kingship first appeared in a story, 'The Phoenix on the Sword', in 1932, and had consumed Howard's final years as the mystically masterful hero of numerous adventures and serials. Oddly enough, Howard seems to have had much in common with the actor who was to immortalize his best-known character.

Born to an adoring mother in Texas in 1906, Howard grew to be a sickly child who turned to body-building in an effort to make something of himself. His fanatical striving for a muscular physique that was nothing short of god-like collided with his other driving force – the urge to write.

By the age of fifteen he had already decided he was a writer, though it was not until he was nineteen that his first piece, 'Spear and Fang', was published. Howard's fame grew with the arrival of another creation, Solomon Kane, and by the late twenties his unstoppable output included straight-down-the-line adventure stories, westerns, oriental extravaganzas and boxing tales, in between which he found time to introduce another favourite barbarian, Kull. For the last four years of his short life it was Conan – a brilliantly-developed Cimmerian savage from the Hyborean Age, vividly sexual and pagan, a barbarian *par excellence* – who proved the dominant figure, featuring in a plethora of brutally sensuous fiction.

Conan's philosophy seemed to match everything that Howard himself wanted to take from life, but real life proved more difficult to cope with. In 1932 Howard's mother fell ill and lapsed into a coma. When Howard was told she would not recover he shot himself. The potency of Conan, however, lived on, as other authors moved in to collect and complete the fund of material Howard had left unfinished, and went on to pen their own sagas of Conan's progress.

It would have been surprising if Hollywood had gone on ignoring the possibilities presented by the Conan stories, but it was not until almost fifty years after Howard's death that a Hollywood movie-man picked up the tab: Edward R. Pressman. Pressman has always been a man who makes movies happen, and has helped many talented newcomers in his industry. Oliver Stone owes a deal to him (Pressman produced his first feature *The Hand* in 1981), Rainer Werner Fassbinder owed his 1981 British debut, *Despair*, to him, while Brian De Palma's *Sisters* and Terrance Malick's *Badlands* (both 1973) were brought into the world by Pressman. His ability to understand the potential of a project and turn it into a box–office package was already proven when he snaffled the rights to Howard's Conan stories, his interest first fired by Ed Summer and George Lucas who introduced Pressman to the Howard-inspired art of Frank Frazetta. According to Pressman, 'the subject was so naturally cinematic, it had to be done'.

Dino De Laurentiis was brought in as producer, and Arnold's name – inevitably – came up for the role of Conan. De Laurentiis was unenthusiastic. The two men had met before. Trying out for the spoof adventure movie *Flash Gordon*, Arnold's brief meeting with his prospective employer had ended when Arnold remarked on what a little man De Laurentiis was.

Arnold's *faux pas* was good news for the blond hunk Sam J. Jones, who was cast as Emperor Ming's *bête noire*, leading the critic Chris Peachment to warn his readers that Jones' Flash is 'thick as a brick, but will no doubt appeal to gentlemen who prefer blonds'. The choice of director John Milius, whose track record included the 1972 screenplay for *The Life and Times of Judge Roy Bean*, the

1973 *Dillinger* and the 1975 *The Wind and the Lion*, both of which he wrote as well as directed, suggested that this was going to be a cut above many other fantasy-based movies. When it became clear that Milius was co-writing with another up-and-coming figure, Oliver Stone, it seemed that at the very least this was going to be an interesting piece.

With Milius in place, Arnold's role in the movie was assured, for Milius could see no alternative and overcame De Laurentiis' objections. The director's autocratic demeanour (the back of his chair was inscribed 'General Milius') didn't lead to his being disliked by those who worked with him, despite his strong views and demanding attitudes. Arnold told Milius that on the day he took office as Governor of California, he would make his new director the Chief of Police. In turn, Milius found that De Laurentiis could be tough and unyielding; it seems to have been a marriage of martinets. Milius' huge commitment to the movie, including a jokey Hitchcockian walk-on role in the market scene, permeated the entire enterprise.

'The great thing is,' said Milius, 'that since Conan's time is prehistory, I was free to make up history, take whatever fascinated me from every early culture I wanted, to mix it all together. In that sense I call this film an historical fantasy rather than an adventure fantasy. I hope to have given this movie a real sense of pagan morality.'

Crucial to the success of the movie was the cinematic recreation of the prose hero, but it must have been obvious to anyone concerned with movies that Arnold might have been born to breathe life into Howard's plaything. Arnold was on the verge of a stunning breakthrough in his career, and knew it.

'When I first heard about *Conan the Barbarian*,' he said, 'I wasn't ready as an actor to play the part. But everything between that time and now, in terms of acting experience, helped prepare me, was a kind of warm up to this.'

Arnold exulted in the extreme physicality of the role, throwing himself into his own stunts while the movie's insurance men looked on aghast. Injuries were inevitable, but seemed necessary if he was to live out Conan's existence. Living it had sometimes to make do for acting it. Milius, who had worked with some of the finest actors in the profession, marshalled the special qualities Arnold could muster by sorting out his various facial expressions and calling on Arnold to come up with the appropriate one for the scene in hand. At the same time, Milius' appreciation of his leading man went even deeper.

'Arnold is one of the great people of the world,' proclaimed Milius. 'I feel it's a great honour just to have known somebody like him. He's not like an actor . . . Arnold's whole philosophy is based around the fact that you have to push so much weight before the muscle grows, and that resistance is good for you.'

Now the savage mastery of Conan found its match in Arnold's wide-screen persona. For Arnold the joy of not feeling afraid permeated his performance; he felt inspired, he said, 'by not being afraid of fearful things'. Here, at least, was an undoubted case of typecasting, and if the critics, whom Arnold knew mattered to his future, might sneer a little ('the male equivalent of the late Jayne Mansfield' smiled Vincent Canby), Arnold knew that his place in the scheme of things had been vindicated by *Conan the Barbarian*, though he realized it was only one stop along a successful journey. 'Look where Ronald Reagan is today,' he said. 'I call that achievement. There is a long, long way to go. I'm only at the beginning.'

The map of Arnold's progress was clear to him. At the close of filming, some of Conan's values and pronouncements seemed to suit Arnold so well that they might have been Arnold's own. 'Let us take the world by the throat and make it give us what we demand' may be Conan's ethos, but now it also had the authentic Arnold ring to it.

Arnold moved to Spain a few weeks before the shoot began there in October 1980, just as *The Jayne Mansfield Story* was playing on TV. Centred around Segovia and Almeria, this was a Spain about to be transformed by Conan's designer, Ron Cobb, whose acclaimed credits included *Aliens* and *Star Wars*. It was Cobb's task to create the Hyborean culture in a span of over sixty exterior and interior settings, including the creation of the boy Conan's village in the snow-covered woody mountains of Valsain. Spain's landscape provided desert enough, but 15,000 cubic metres of sand had to be shifted to create three great sand-hills for one important sequence. The ability to move mountains seemed the least anyone involved in this $22,400,000 movie could manage.

The boy Conan is brought up, via an opening scene that suggests all the grandeur of a Cecil B. De Mille prologue, to live by his sword-maker father's trust in steel. Thulsa Doom and his deadly army sweep into his village, rasing it to the ground and executing Conan's parents. Thulsa's symbol – the two snakes that are one, facing each other – is imprinted on the boy's mind.

Taken prisoner and put to the wheel, the years of Conan's enslavement drag on into manhood, but this hard labour, ironically, helps Conan to develop his brilliant physique. Thrust into a pit as the ready victim of a vicious fighter, Conan uses brute force to destroy his opponent and becomes a well-known pit fighter, mercilessly battering those thrown into the ground to face him. A sense of his own worth begins to dawn on him.

To further his education he is sent to the East, where he is instructed in the wisdom of the war masters; poetry, philosophy and the enjoyment of supple women are part of the curriculum. At last, he is set free and runs who knows where, falling into a cave where he discovers the sword of Crom, whose long-dead bones disintegrate before him. Moving on, Conan is seduced by a sultry woman who, with Conan inside her, transmogrifies into a terrifying harpy – another manifestation of Crom. Conan teams up with a thief and archer and proves his barbarian tendencies by punching a camel full in the face, but his gentler emotions are exposed when he meets the Queen of Thieves, Valeria (Sandahl Bergman) and they fall deeply in love with one another.

They are taken to the hall of King Osric the Usurper (Max von Sydow), now feeble and care-worn, who tells Conan that Thulsa Doom has stolen his daughter. Commanded to return her to her grieving father, Conan rides off to infiltrate Thulsa's domain. Disguised as a pilgrim (so convincingly and attractively that a lustful elder priest tries to seduce him) Conan comes close to Thulsa, but is recognized as an infidel, and brought in custody before the evil ruler. Thulsa explains to Conan that flesh is stronger than steel as, at his bidding, a girl throws herself from a great height to fall at his feet, and is killed. Condemned to crucifixion, Conan is put upon the Tree of Woe, where death waits to claim him, until, over the hills, come his rescuers. Demons struggle to take his soul but, with some intervention by a diminutive wizard and a desperate attempt by Valeria to fight off the spirits trying to take him into the next world, Conan survives to fight another day.

Restored to tremendous physical strength and sense of purpose, Conan leads his little posse to Thulsa's kingdom, where they arrive in time to witness a lethargic orgy presided over by Thulsa himself, who slowly transmutes into a gigantic snake. The thieves take Osric's daughter and make their getaway, but Thulsa, returned to human form, makes an arrow out of a snake and pierces the escaping Valeria, who dies in Conan's arms. Her death is the final turn of the screw in Conan's determination to avenge the loss of those he has loved. In one final confrontation, Thulsa tells Conan that he has now become his father, just as he is father to the countless thousands of pilgrims come to worship him. In answer, Conan hacks Thulsa to the ground and sets fire to the palace as the people turn in obeisance to their new idol. Conan rules.

Released in the US on 14 May 1982, *Conan the Barbarian* took almost $10 million over its first weekend, and went on to gross $21,700,000 – not even clearing its production costs. It seemed easy enough for some to scoff at the movie. After comparing Arnold to Jayne Mansfield, Vincent Canby went on to describe his new film as 'a kiddie fantasy for grown-ups', but perhaps he was in an unresponsive mood that day. We are certainly presented with a confused and disjointed screenplay, and some poor delineation of the major characters, but *Conan the Barbarian* can lay several claims to being some sort of work of art.

Visually the film is a delight, thanks mainly to the work of Ron Cobb and photographer Duke Callaghan. Cobb's version of the Hyborean Age would surely have satisfied Robert E. Howard himself, for it looks exactly like the real thing would have looked like had it ever existed, down to the preposterous helmets of Thulsa Doom's men, looking like leftovers from Orson Welles' cheapjack movie of

Macbeth. Both director and camera seem to have been looking at the actors at the precise moment when something special was happening to their performances.

The first moment that we see Conan the man, his face slowly moving upwards from the wheel he has turned throughout childhood, adolescence and young manhood, is a tellingly effective way not only of establishing Conan's strength, but also the potency of Arnold's peculiar charisma (if we didn't know before this moment that Arnold meant to make it big in films, he tells us so with that one piercing look). The killing of Conan's mother is as good an example of Milius' huge care as any other, in a scene that is a masterclass in still acting, while Thulsa Doom's transformation scene, managed without any special effects, is truly chilling. Throughout, Basil Poledouris' audacious score helps things along splendidly, whether it is sounding like Carl Orff's 'Carmina Burana' or Borodin's 'Polotsvian Dances'.

Everything combines to make the final show-down between Conan and Thulsa Doom the pay-off of the movie, but it is an achievement that worried the critic Roger Ebert, made uncomfortable by the almost ritual slaughter of the black villain by the white hero. ' I found myself thinking,' said Ebert, 'that Leni Reifenstahl could have directed the scene, and that Goebbels might have applauded it.' Ebert's concerns may seem a little over-refined in a situation where the actor playing Thulsa Doom merely happens to be black, but for comfort's sake Milius might have considered this aspect more carefully.

Many intelligent critics were unimpressed by the work. 'Whatever their mythological pretences,' wrote Richard Combs for the *Monthly Film Bulletin*, 'its characters are cut from the dullest comic-book material, and neither his Christ-like tribulations (what would Nietzsche have thought of this?) nor the Oedipal nature of his revenge lend much dimension to Schwarzenegger's Conan . . . [The film's] anti-liberal brief is severely limited, while as straightforward sword and sorcery it is a crashing bore.'

It seems almost frightening, but Arnold was at one time committed to the possibility of making five Conan pictures for Dino De

Laurentiis; it turned out as three – at least two too many for most of his admirers. As it happened, neither John Milius or Oliver Stone could find the time or interest to get involved with *Conan the Destroyer* (1984), for which a more prosaic script was prepared by Stanley Mann, to be directed by the veteran Richard Fleischer. It was ultimately his responsibility to make sure the new movie was more than a warming-over of its prequel. Figuring that bigger might in this case mean better, Fleischer made a start by asking Arnold, as he watched him stripped for sword-play in preparation for the film, to put on extra muscles, which he obligingly did.

Whatever the qualities of *Conan the Destroyer*, Arnold looked physically superb when shooting began in Samalayuca, Mexico, in November 1983. This time around, De Laurentiis had set up a budget of $18 million, $4 million less than had been spent on the first Conan project. Not exactly encouraging news, perhaps, but it could be argued that the new movie was altogether gentler, more hybrid than the first. It also boasted a considerable, striking leading lady in singer Grace Jones, impersonating a female barbarian, Zula, easily a match for any Conan. Arnold and his co-star got on well together, despite her penchant for hitting those unlucky enough to be standing close by over the head with a stick. 'She's wild,' said Arnold. 'Fantastic. We admired each other right away, and she's become a good pal of mine.'

In the new film Conan is mixed up in a Snow White-type plot, for he is to escort the delightfully pert Princess Jehnna (played by fifteen-year-old Olivia D'Abo) to obtain a key and magical horn for the seemingly kindly Queen Taramis (Sarah Douglas), in effect the Wicked Queen, who means to use the horn to revive the god Dagoth, and then have Conan and the Princess murdered. Taramis sends her black henchman Bombaata (played by the basketball star, Wilt 'The Stilt' Chamberlain) apparently to assist the adventurers, but in reality to spy and murder. The thief and wizard from *Conan the Barbarian* join the posse, as does the capably violent Zula (Jones), and they help their master to overcome all obstacles, until Dagoth rears up terrifyingly, loses control, and annihilates Taramis and her followers.

Mann's treatment was said at the time to bring a more casual, homey atmosphere into the Conan stories, and several critics found the lighter tone and lack of pretension more appealing than in the Milius original. Richard Combs now thought it almost a relief 'to find nothing primal, Oedipal, Nietzschean or survivalist creasing the hero's brow in the second instalment, just a straight rerun B Western'. As for Arnold, 'Let's face it,' said Roger Ebert, 'the Conan series does not require extraordinary acting ability, although Schwarzenegger provides a sound professional centre to the story, and the film would be impossible if he couldn't carry off Conan . . . They're repackaging Conan as your friendly family barbarian.'

Taking $14,300,000, the movie proved another loser for De Laurentiis, but not enough of a clinker to put him off pushing Arnold into another sword-and-sorcery picture. Today the warm notices for *Conan the Destroyer* seem as puzzling as the dreadful ones for *Conan the Barbarian*, for it comes across as tepid stuff. The pluses include some good costumes, charm from the young D'Abo, a nicely anorexic leer from Jones, and some glimpses of a more humane Conan. Against this there is the plodding screenplay, dull lighting, cheesy special effects (including a particularly disappointing rubbery Dagoth made by the creator of *E.T.*, Carlo Rambaldi), and the sneaky feeling that everything was done so much better in the first movie.

Perhaps one of the reasons why Arnold survived Dino De Laurentiis and the almost ludicrous macho qualities of poor old Conan is that somehow, despite his sometimes overbearing tendency to be just as macho in real life, Arnold persisted in showing the sort of understanding that might not have been expected of him. One of the most telling examples of a perhaps unexpected philosophy was emphasized in his welcome and tolerant attitude to gay issues. 'It's the greatest compliment you can have, to be found attractive by both sexes. Why should I mind?' he asked in 1979.

He had once found himself sharing space in a public bathhouse with a well-known maker of gay porn movies. John Doe walked up to Arnold, introduced himself, told Arnold he was gay, and asked if he could watch him take his shower. Arnold didn't even think of objecting. 'It would have been stupid for me to have minded about that, he was so open and free about it.'

As well as opposing Anita Bryant's virulent anti-homosexual campaign throughout America, Arnold was also very much aware of the stance taken in Britain by Mary Whitehouse and her followers on gay issues. 'Where do they get their energy from?' he wondered. 'If I were prepared to spend so much energy against one particular group of people I'd start to ask myself why. I'm too busy doing the things I wanted to do. I haven't the energy to hate.'

These are not the views we might expect from so masculine an icon as Arnold, and they show a refreshing breadth of understanding. There is a suspicion, too, that Arnold's broad-mindedness may have been reinforced by his years in the inevitably male-dominated world of body-building where, as Wendy Leigh's book accentuates, the slur of furtive homosexuality has always lurked. Arnold is not unaware of this, but stresses that the homosexual element was introduced by the sport's voyeurs. Naturally, there were always girls offering to cover him with chocolate and lick it off, but 'You get the guys as well. They come round the gym and watch you work out, then send a note to say they will pay $1,000 dollars if you sleep with them . . . In all my career I have only met two body-builders who were homosexual.'

7 Touches of Evil

From hero to villain, from film actor to superstar – the first a gamble, the second a matter of timing – *The Terminator* launched Arnold into the stratosphere of his profession. Vilified though it might be for its violence – in 1993 it must have been one of the most cited examples of harmful violence on offer to the public – it was a devastatingly astute choice for the muscleman of the cinema to make, and has continued to confuse audiences and critics (including many who condemn it without having sat through it), waiting perhaps for the day when it will be revealed as a witty, inspired and innovative piece of film-making.

The Terminator was the brainchild of husband- and wife-to-be team James Cameron and Gale Anne Hurd, both of whom had seen service with the doyen of feature film directors (and budget-minded producers), Roger Corman of New World Pictures. Hurd had worked as Corman's executive assistant, and subsequently as the company's publicity director, working with the penny-pinching maestro on such movies as *The Lady in Red* and *Alligator*. As well as co-writing *The Terminator*, Hurd would now act as producer to her husband's director on what would be only his second main feature, the previous having been an undistinguished effort, *Piranha 2*.

The truth was that Cameron already had superb grounding in his industry, with credits in various departments. He had supervised the special effects for *Escape from New York*, been production designer and second unit director for New World's distinctive *Planet of Horrors*, and worked as art director and director of photography for special effects on *Battle Beyond the Stars*.

If Cameron had gone along with his first ideas about Arnold the fate of the movie might have been very different, for the director offered him the role of Kyle Reese, the guerrilla-fighter hero from another time who comes to earth to combat the evil of the Terminator, and Cameron must surely be forgiven for imagining that no star of the stature of Arnold would want to play an out-and-out villain whose inhumanity was stronger simply because he was inhuman. If it was Arnold alone who perceived Cameron's error, we need little more evidence to single him out as one of the most perceptive of actors.

Far from wanting to represent the power of good, Arnold told Cameron he wanted to play the Terminator him- (or it-) self, and clung to his belief despite advice to the contrary. By the time the movie appeared it was obvious that, far from taking the wrong path, Arnold had effectively used the film to help reinvent himself; it proved a revelation to audiences and critics, marking Arnold as the force he had always intended to be.

Arnold's reinvention could not have been more artfully achieved. With *The Terminator*, he marks the end of those films where his body is the *raison d'être*, where any swollen muscle-bound hopeful might have stepped in to take over, though there would still be movies that stressed his structure rather than his talent. It might not have seemed this way from the opening shot of Arnold, kneeling in what we might take as a pose used by the great Sandow himself, but muscles play a very secondary part in the film, and beyond them is an intellectually stimulating and heart-warming movie, in which Arnold perfectly understands his participation.

The boldness of the movie is not merely that Arnold has now turned robotic villain, whose mission is to kill without question, without remorse, even if with a good deal of reason. Whatever he was concerned about in taking the role, it was clearly not a loss of audience sympathy, though to the innocent it might be thought he was courting disaster in turning down the role of male saviour, with its human interest and heart-tugging qualities, for the role of a mindless murderer with only a few snatches of dialogue.

What Arnold understood was the importance of the image in cinema, where words might not be the vital thing (though when few are used, they had better be good). If we consider some of the cinema's most potent and enduring reincarnations of evil – Frankenstein's monster, the Golem, Nosferatu – we observe that it is our visual understanding of them that keeps them alive and vibrant and frightful in our minds, for they are creatures of very few words (though Count Dracula, exceptionally, is almost a charming conversationalist). And was not Arnold already a master of the wordless image, through body-building? His voice did not matter, to the extent that when his body became well-known enough to be thrust into *Hercules Goes Bananas* audiences were presumably none the wiser that a stentorian actor had dubbed his dialogue.

Much, too, had already been made of the Schwarzenegger humour, an innate, sometimes slightly cruel, wit that came happily off the screen. It had been developed in *Stay Hungry* and *Pumping Iron*, submerged in *The Villain* and *The Jayne Mansfield Story*, and noticed by those who wanted to discover it in the Conan movies, but it is really in *The Terminator* that we first catch sight of a witty actor.

Unfortunately the wit would lie dormant for the next two films, but during test screenings for *The Terminator* it was not surprising that audiences found the unforced, subtle humour of Arnold's scenes among the most appealing. This is despite the fact that, according to Arnold, 'In *The Terminator* there was some indirect humour, but it wasn't written for that, that was just the reaction of the people.'

Cameron and Hurd's strokes are so delicate that the laughs in no way detract from the violent thrust of the action or the seriousness of the underlying theme; they are a part of a well integrated whole, just as Una O'Connor's brilliant hysterics, worked into such classics as *The Bride of Frankenstein* and *The Invisible Man*, enhance the horror that is all around her. The narrative drive in *The Terminator* is also distinguished by the three principal roles, from which only the heroine survives to the end of the story, the hero's death having been followed by that of the Terminator. In his death is another deft touch, for although Arnold vanishes from the final pages of the screenplay, being reduced for the closing scenes to his skeletal workings, the strength of the image he has created, now determinedly crawling towards his prey, is not diminished.

When it comes to the importance of image, we can see that

Arnold has the natural qualities of a Karloff or a Lugosi, and must keep our fingers crossed that, unlike them, he does not move away from his achievement into a lifetime's struggle against increasingly feeble screenplays, second-rate directors and plain daft movies (though any half-awake reader will already know that there is little chance of this ever happening to our Arnold).

For Cameron, *The Terminator*'s beginnings may lie in his belief that 'I've never really seen a good robot in a movie, ever, not a really great one the way they used to be portrayed on the covers of *Analog*, whose robots had a waist like an insect so you knew it could not be a guy in a suit.' The idea was probably stirred by several sources, not least the work of Harlan Ellison, who took action against Cameron's company for plagiarising his story 'I have no Mouth but I can Scream', and allegedly an episode from TV's *The Outer Limits* series entitled 'Demon with a Glass Hand'.

Ellison was awarded an out-of-court settlement, and has his name credited on currently available prints of the movie, but looking over Ellison's shoulder we can see that *The Terminator* owes much to several movies that have gone before. We also find echoes of the work of Philip K. Dick, notably his story 'Second Variety', about the introduction into a war-weary society of mass-produced robots who have every appearance of human beings.

Modestly budgeted at $6.5 million (a sum its sequel would multiply several times over), *The Terminator* is a contained, almost home-spun effort compared to some of the megabuck movies Arnold would involve himself in later in his career. Ultimately the effectiveness of Cameron and Hurd's brainchild lay in the directness of its storyline, based on the brilliant concept of the manoeuvrability of time, the fact that the future, though prescribed, can be diverted, upset and even altered. This is both the film's strength and its success.

We are shown an apocalyptic, scaled-down vision of the world-to-be in 2029, denuded of everything civilized and civilizing, where machines rule by terror and force. Into the urban nightmare of present-day America come two crouching figures, embryo-like in their posing nudity until they arise and vanish into the streets: the

Terminator (Arnold) and Kyle Reese (Michael Biehn). The first may stand for evil and the second for good, but both have come from that terrible future glimpsed in the film's opening moments, and both have the same mission, to find Sarah Connor (Linda Hamilton).

The Terminator's task is to exterminate Sarah, for it is her as-yet-unborn (indeed, unthought-of) son who will become the Messiah who leads the world away from the abyss and overthrows the tyranny of the machines, the Terminator and his masters. The Terminator's hit-and-miss attempts to eliminate the correct Sarah Connor result in the bloody and unnecessary deaths of several innocents before it lights on its real quarry, beginning the frantic chase that thrusts the movie forward.

The truths facing Sarah involve her in great leaps of understanding, when Reese tells her he has been sent to earth by her son, John Connor, who will bring the world back from the after-effects of a cataclysmic nuclear holocaust, in the aftermath of which men and machines fight for supremacy. But Sarah is not a mother and has not yet met the man who would make motherhood a possibility; as if this were not enough she finds herself lacking any of the qualities she supposes the mother of a saviour should possess. Relentlessly the Terminator searches, killing as he goes, sometimes (as in the much-quoted scene at the police-station) offering some sort of warning of his intentions. Getting no satisfaction from the desk-sergeant, the Terminator tells him 'I'll be back', walks out, grabs a truck and ploughs it through the building.

Such escapades convince Sarah that Reese knows what he is talking about, and she finds comfort when he shows her the photograph of herself that John has given him, a photograph Reese has come to love, finding in his leader's mother the extraordinary strength and goodness that begins to be other-worldly, that has its own strength. Elected to be the mother of a Christ-like hero, Sarah inevitably takes on the role of a latter-day streetwise Virgin Mary.

When their mutual beauty, respect and awe make Reese and Sarah's love-making inevitable, we see that Reese, as a man from the next century, makes possible what is in effect an immaculate conception. Yet their night of love turns into another morning of realization that the Terminator is hard on their heels. Escaping in a pickup truck from the motel where John has been conceived, Reese and Sarah are chased by the Terminator on a motorcycle, who then commandeers a tanker truck. Reese blows it up, but is himself killed. From the flames creep the metallic skeletal remains of the Terminator, never a quitter, but Sarah eventually manages to crush him to death in a hydraulic press. Made richer, quieter and more secure in the knowledge of her destiny, and the destiny of her unborn son, a pregnant Sarah leaves the horror behind and drives out into the desert where, some months later, a small boy insists on taking a Polaroid snapshot of her. It is the same photograph that John Connor will give to Kyle Reese.

Here, Arnold is involved in a deceptively entertaining movie that works on many levels, allowing even those with the most limited gung-ho sensibilities to feel satisfied with the apparently unending mayhem and destruction. *The Terminator* is sometimes dismissed as offering no more than this, but this is a nonsense, for at the movie's core is a life-enhancing surge of proper feeling, eternal morality and the ascendancy of what is real and good.

If we have a film that carries such a potentially portentous message, we are also beguiled by the deftness of its 'time' elements, making what might be unlikely or physically impossible somehow mystical, so that when the film ends on its stabbingly sentimental note of hope we are aware of three journeys followed to their different conclusions. *The Terminator*'s final poetic justice is that the Terminator is himself terminated, while Reese is sacrificed rather than killed. As for Sarah's journey, hers has been the most difficult and inspiring, from hometown waitress, little Miss Ordinary America, to Virgin Mother. If not exactly Feminist Film of the Year, *The Terminator* does, through Sarah's toughness and determination, have an emancipatory ring about it.

So much that is valuable about *The Terminator* is better appreciated when seen as the background for its sequel, an occasion marked by Cameron's unswerving belief in the efficacy of his original story. Here, for once, is a follow-up that takes no easy options, that presses no repeat buttons, but storms ahead with its own momentum. With its massively swollen budget and state-of-the-art special effects, the sequel is obviously the louder of the two movies, building on the qualities of the first, and making the most of the dramatic coup that has Arnold changing sides, proving that even Terminators can be good. Though it might be thought that in creating this *volte-face* Cameron and Arnold were taking the easy cutesey path to lovability, *Terminator 2* grows naturally out of its predecessor.

Looking over his shoulder to Sylvester Stallone, Arnold felt confident that his rival's crown was far from secure. Between *Rocky III* in 1982 and *Rambo: First Blood Part II* in 1985 had come the John Travolta semi-musical *Staying Alive* (1983) and another semi-musical, disastrously teaming Sly with Dolly Parton, *Rhinestone* (1984). Stallone had not strained for the quality of work that, according to Arnold at least, was the bedrock of Arnold's career. Stallone's films, despite their star's physical glory, concentrated on the weakness of human strength (excluding the Rambo movies) and the frailty of emotions (including the Rambo movies). *The Terminator* showed once and for all that there was something superhuman about the image Arnold successfully promulgated on screen.

He had also explored genre untouched by his rivals. Science fiction or futuristic films provided golden opportunities for gargantuan budgets, mind-boggling effects, unending invention and, implicit in all good futuristic movies, a kind of message. Here was Arnold's finest hour to date, over which he had more control than any other movie he had yet made, and to which he brought that presence that is not quite acting, the image that persists despite a lack of dialogue.

Speaking of the film in 1991, Arnold said 'It took me from the Conan-like parts that were being offered to me because of my body . . . and created good box-office. And that sent a whole new signal out to the community. I think *The Terminator* made people think . . . It was understood that I had the body, but I didn't have to show it to make a point.'

Taking $17 million in the USA alone, the quality of *The Terminator* was generally recognized, even if it was perceived in some quarters as little more than yet another violent, all-action vehicle for its star. For the *Monthly Film Bulletin* Julian Petley thought that 'one should note the excellence of Schwarzenegger's first role as a heavy . . . in which his sheer physical presence evokes the Terminator's remorseless momentum' and considered the picture 'an exemplary piece of virtuoso, high-tech exploitation movie-making', while Chris Peachment for *Time Out* wrote that it had 'more than enough violence to make it a moral film, and Arnold's a whizz'.

8   Surviving Conan

Arnold's contractual arrangements with De Laurentiis explain why he played a supporting role, though credited as the star, in what was effectively his third Conan picture. What were his, and Conan's, admirers, to make of this new epic? Arnold looked and behaved just like Conan, in a story that was unmistakably Conan-centred, but now he pretended to be playing a barbaric goody, a High Lord or some such nonsense, called Kalidor. This was hardly the character the film's audience was supposed to remember, having had its eponymous heroine, Red Sonja, drummed into its consciousness time and again throughout the movie. For Red Sonja read Brigitte Nielsen, the leggy, temperamental, ambitious Swedish model who had her sights set on Hollywood. Hers was a name that Arnold would come to know well.

Born in 1963 of a librarian mother and engineer father, Brigitte had worn teeth-braces as a child and had a gawky, awkward way with her through her adolescence. Her life had changed dramatically by the age of seventeen, when she was already in demand as a top fashion model, travelling across the world for photography sessions. She settled in Milan as the partner of the agent Lucca Rossi, but then married a Copenhagen musician by whom she had a son, Julian. Brigitte's original choice of name for the boy, Sylvester (after the film actor she had idolized and written undelivered letters to throughout her developing years), was overruled by her husband.

Shortly after giving birth to the boy Brigitte came to the notice of De Laurentiis, who was noisily searching Europe for an actress to play the lead in his up-and-coming movie, and who offered Brigitte the contract. She accepted, and launched out on a brief but hectic schedule of movies, in some of which Sylvester Stallone – the actor she had been fixed on for years – was to feature.

For Brigitte, *Red Sonja* was a strong beginning to a career she meant to pursue with speed and determination. The films followed fast on one another's heels. When *Red Sonja* was in the can and she and Arnold had ended their friendship, Stallone hastily wrote her into his *Rocky IV* (1985) as a hard-nut Russian official. She was Stallone's co-star in *Cobra* (1986), meeting her real-life lover Stallone in on-screen love scenes that were, according to one critic, like 'waiting for giant pandas to mate'. *Beverly Hills Cop II* (1987) had her as its villainess, although the press preferred to concentrate on stories of her relationship with its star and director. By the time Brigitte got around to making *Domino* (1989), almost everybody seemed to have lost interest in her career.

When she arrived in Rome during September 1984 to begin work on *Red Sonja*, however, Brigitte's hopes were high. It was Arnold who became the centre of her attention, her co-star and in effect her supporting player despite having his name over the marquee. In a curious and tactless way De Laurentiis had ousted Arnold from his throne and replaced him with a new, female, equivalent. Never afraid of giving his customers too much of a good thing, De Laurentiis now offered not one but two foreign stars, two heavy accents, two superbly developed bodies for the price of one.

Thrown together in such circumstances, it might not have been surprising had Arnold resented having the new-found actress around. During the early days of filming he stressed that their relationship would be purely professional, but it soon became clear that Arnold and Brigitte made an attractive couple and she became his frequent escort and companion. The truth was that Brigitte was infatuated with Arnold, and her professional relationship with him was a curious one. She, a tyro star, was headlining a film in which one of Hollywood's legends was playing second fiddle.

Aurelia visited the set of *Red Sonja* and was not pleased with the company Arnold was keeping; she did not want to see Brigitte replacing Maria as her daughter-in-law. Meanwhile Maria became aware of Brigitte's affair with Arnold, charted in some detail by the

Vienna Kurier, though the American press were either innocent of or unwilling to expose what was going on. Meanwhile there was a film to be made.

Director Richard Fleischer had the misfortune to be hired for *Red Sonja* immediately after *Conan the Destroyer*, a daunting prospect for the man responsible for such disparately entertaining pieces as *Doctor Doolittle* (1967) and the nastily efficient *10 Rillington Place* (1970).

As for the screenplay, Clive Exton and George Macdonald Fraser failed to come up with a single decent line. In a prologue we learn that our heroine's parents were slaughtered (shades of Conan's childhood) by evil Queen Gedren (Sandahl Bergman, Conan's lover from *Conan the Barbarian*) and her vicious army, which also violated poor Sonja. Understandably put out, Sonja slashed Gedren's face and, years later, is granted strength and purpose by a visiting vapour cloud of a Fairy Godmother who tells Sonja that she will achieve justice and vengeance.

Gedren now seeks the talisman. a glowing green ball with vast powers, with which she knows she will be able to control the destiny of the earth. The wicked trinket is due to be destroyed by a gathering of virgin-white priestesses, assisted by the he-man Kalidor (Arnold), when Gedren's troops intervene, slaughtering the brave maidens and wresting the talisman from them. Varna (Janet Agren) manages to escape and stumbles, dying, into Kalidor's arms, telling him to call in her sister Red Sonja. Far away, Sonja is busy brushing up her sword-play technique with her Japanese master ('You have no more to learn, Red Sonja. Never have I seen your equal') when Kalidor fetches her to her dying sister. Varna tells Sonja of the talisman's dangerous power which feeds on the light; in thirteen days it will be strong enough to destroy the world. Varna dies. Kalidor offers to help Sonja in her quest, but is refused, for Sonja needs the help of no man (and thus Arnold's role is neatly set aside, allowing him only to appear, like the cavalry, at high moments of tension when female grit may not be enough to save the day). Such independence may be admirable, but we are still not spared Sonja and Kalidor being attracted to one another, their devotion marked by one or two incredibly tame romantic clinches.

The adventure, if such it can be called, meanders on. Allies are gained (a pompous boy prince and his portly, put-upon retainer), enemies are defeated (the brutal Brytag by Sonja, a ridiculous sea-monster by Kalidor), until Sonja is at last able to face Gedren who has gone wildly out of control, as has her beloved talisman. Sonja slays Gedren and consigns the talisman to eternity as Sonja falls into Kalidor's arms.

Red Sonja might have been saved by one or two reasonable performances, but they are not in evidence. Sandahl Bergman, so effective as Conan's lover, is all at sea here, lumbered with some ridiculous lines, while Janet Agren's death scene is splendidly awful. The little prince is kept busy being cute, and has some truly embarrassing scenes with Brigitte.

Fleischer made agreeable noises about the talents of De Laurentiis' newly discovered leading lady, but there is precious little sign of any warmth or natural ebullience from Brigitte, who looks sullen throughout. In her debut she gives the impression that acting is a one-dimensional exercise. It would be gratifying to find Arnold saving the film with a performance worthy of a weathered professional, but *Red Sonja* is surely Arnold's most feeble outing. His heart is not in it, and may have had troubles of its own. What he *is* able to bring to the movie is his presence, which is as strong as his infrequent appearances allow. The softness of his make-up belies the apparent toughness of Kalidor, giving Arnold the blush of some mighty Nureyev, but when it comes to the business of acting Arnold's contribution is negligible. *Red Sonja* was nobody's finest hour.

Commando, Arnold's next movie, at least attracted a proper sort of attention for its male star, but *Commando*'s fate was to be too often compared unfavourably with the Rambo movies (Arnold coming across the inescapable Stallone yet again).

On the face of it there is something in this criticism. Both heroes are one-time highly-skilled killing soldiers now sheltering in a peaceful environment, only to be plucked from it into the maelstrom of new bloody conflict. Both heroes go in for a deal of legalized slaughter; both leave their respective battlefields unbowed but insistent that never again will they return. In Stallone's case there is also a strong suspicion that regret, even anguish, has entered his soul. Arnold is more clear-minded, and did whatever he could not to have his work compared with that of his adversary. '[Stallone's] is a very politically oriented movie and mine is not at all. Mine is humour oriented. You can laugh and you can have a good time with it and I don't take myself seriously in the film either. I believe in comic relief, otherwise the whole thing becomes too intense and too heavy.'

For *Commando* Arnold's director was Mark L. Lester, whose earlier work included *Truck Stop Women* (1974), a flavoursome cult movie boasting such unlikely names as Lieux Dressler, Dolores Dorn and Dennis Fimple, and *Class of 84* (1981) with Perry King in the role originated by Glenn Ford in this rerun of the 1955 *The Blackboard Jungle*. Producer Joel Silver, making a speciality of all-action movies, went on to co-produce Arnold's *Predator*. At the head of the supporting cast the young Canadian actress Rae Dawn Chong was signed as Arnold's companion in adventure, while Australian actor Vernon Wells, who had memorably lent support to Mel Gibson in the futuristic *The Road Warrior* (1982) as Wes 'Mad Dog' Bikerider, was cast as his adversary.

Steven E. de Souza, who went on to write *The Running Man*, contrived a screenplay that sometimes managed to balance fast action and violence with humour. Retired ace soldier Colonel Matrix (Arnold) is living contentedly in a comfortable hideaway among remote hills with his young daughter Jenny (Alyssa Milano). She is kidnapped by the psychotic Bennett (Wells), once one of Matrix's men and now bent on revenge against Matrix, the commander who had him thrown out of the force, though we never quite know why.

Bennett tells Matrix that Jenny will be released when Matrix assassinates the democratically-elected President of Val Verde, a country once ruled over by the torturing despot General Arius (Dan Hedaya) for whom Bennett now works. Matrix is seen onto a plane which will take him to his destination, but escapes and instigates a campaign of elimination to get to Jenny, assisted by an innocent bystander at a shopping mall, Cindy (Chong), who gets involved in the imbroglio. Ultimately, his face painted for combat, Matrix goes on an orgy of killing as he storms the island fortress where Jenny is held, finally coming to the inevitable one-to-one confrontation with Bennett. Bennett, of course, loses the contest, enjoying his final glimpses of Matrix as he impales him on a phallic object, leaving Matrix to be reunited with his girlfriend and the freed Jenny.

The components of success are all here: deftly directed action sequences after a brief, peaceful prologue of Matrix and Jenny enjoying their ideal life together; some agreeable supporting performances; a superb score from James Horner; a screenplay stuffed with one-liners for the star (asked what has happened to a man he was holding over a precipice, Arnold replies 'I let him go'). The relationship between Matrix and Cindy is sassy enough, but hardly the rollicking comedy we might have expected. The development of Arnold's screen persona relies on the fact that his killing mission is simply because of his love for his young daughter, with whom he has an idyllic relationship. Arnold is particularly effective in the opening scenes, showing a gentler and more domestic side, until the grenades begin to be unpinned; there is a naturalness about him that is striking. These advances in technique seemed to come quite naturally to him. 'I'm not the kind of actor that likes to make a big effort in getting into the character,' he claimed. 'I like to creep up on it, slowly, and then all of a sudden be in it. When I get the job, I start preparing myself for the film as I go along, as I study the script. I start reading a lot of material about this kind of character.'

The demands of the screenplay on Arnold are considerable, but the feeling, once the action gets under way, that we should be laughing at the torture and the slaughter gets in the way. With no consistency about the style, what are we supposed to find funny? It is not only the hero and heroine who are allowed to be funny in this movie, but also the villains – is this intentional?

Vernon Wells makes a very pot-bellied nasty, his paunch encased in chain-mail and leather, a somewhat risible arch-criminal. Despite his unpleasant dialogue and permanently evil leer, Bennett remains a comic-book character. The final collision between Bennett and Matrix is so laden with homo-erotic sado-machochistic overtones, made absurd by Wells' portly advances, that we smile rather than tense, are engaged rather than repulsed. The rest of Bennett's claque (tinpot despot with a desperately Italian accent, weedy little thug, etc.) are familiar types with stock responses.

For Kim Newman in *Monthly Film Bulletin*, Arnold was 'the perfect embodiment of the reactionary superman ideal evoked by Rambo and Chuck Norris'. For this critic Arnold 'seems to have lost the insouciance he displayed when appearing as himself in *Pumping Iron*, and his handling of the James Bond-style grim wise-cracks . . . is disappointingly lumpen'.

Arnold seems to have been pleased with his work on *Commando*: 'It's great when I watch the dailies and look at myself, and I can comfortably say it was really good. Normally you don't like to see the dailies when they're unedited. This film was the first time where I could comfortably watch them, and really feel that I'd made a great step forward with my acting.'

Such professional success was played out alongside Arnold's home life, which now threatened to become all blueberry pie. His Americanization had been confirmed when he became a citizen of the United States on 16 September 1983, but it was two years later, on 10 August 1985, that his links with America were immeasurably strengthened with the announcement of his engagement to Maria Shriver. By the end of the year, Arnold was making grand plans for the coming event, which included the purchase of a $5 million mansion at Pacific Palisades.

Since *The Terminator* Arnold's work had scarcely been distinguished, a trend continued by his next effort, *Raw Deal*, which began shooting in Chicago during November 1985. Workmanlike, it is a tired product of the Dino De Laurentiis stable. Noises made at the time by the production company promised 'a more expanded acting role' for Arnold, but any progression is at best cosmetic in a vehicle that effectively strait-jackets its star. More might have been expected of the director, British-born John Irvin, who had moved on from early work with London Transport Films to such movies as *Turtle Diary* (1985), about a children's author (Glenda Jackson) and an unassuming clerk (Ben Kingsley) freeing turtles from London Zoo. Alas, nothing so exciting happens in *Raw Deal*.

The 'expanded' role for Arnold is that of Mark Kaminski, a one-time successful cop with the FBI, who resigned after being accused of gross violence by the ratty Federal prosecutor Baxter (Joe Regalbuto). Kaminski, we know, is at least two-thirds innocent, since his victim was a child molester, rapist and murderer. The ex-FBI bright boy is now a small-time sheriff coping with an alcoholic wife (Blanche Baker). Sick of their dull life together, she pipes the word 'Shit' across a chocolate cake. Kaminski tells her, 'You should not drink and bake.'

Kaminski's old boss, Harry Shannon (Darren McGavin), hires him to infiltrate the kingdom of ruthless gang leader Luigi Patrovita (Sam Wanamaker), responsible for the death of Shannon's policeman-son. Kaminski kills himself off, assumes a new identity, and romances with Monique (Kathryn Harrold), who at first acts as informant on him to Patrovita. Soon, of course, she is falling for Kaminski or, as he is now known, Joe P. Brenner (The 'P' stands, apparently, for Pussy). Kaminski gets himself taken on as a leading henchman for Patrovita, hoping to replace Max (Robert Davi), who not only has the hots for Monique but later learns Brenner's true identity, and sets him up to kill Shannon. At the last moment Kaminski realizes the trap, but Max shoots Shannon anyway, and Kaminski kills Max.

It is now finale time. Arnold dresses with almost bridal vanity in his hugging white t-shirt, arming himself with a vast arsenal before setting out to eliminate his enemies. He wipes out an army of them as the soundtrack screams out the Rolling Stones' 'I Can't Get No Satisfaction'. Patrovita and his assistant, Rocca (Paul Shenar), perish by his hand. A cringing Baxter is the only crook left crawling after the slaughter, and Kaminski hands him a gun, advising him to 'Resign or be prosecuted.' A bad egg to the last, Baxter goes to shoot Kaminski in the back, but Kaminski kills him.

Mission accomplished, Kaminski gets back with the FBI and his now happily pregnant and presumably off-the-bottle wife. He visits the crippled Shannon who, with his friend's encouragement, takes his first faltering steps towards recovery, falling contentedly into Kaminski's arms. Freeze frame.

Released in the USA on 6 June 1986, *Raw Deal* went on to take $7 million at the box-office. The weakest film Arnold had made

since *The Terminator*, its critical reception was not altogether nega-
tive though few threw their hats in the air. David Denby wrote that
Arnold 'tried to be debonair in John Irvin's nifty, semi-satirical
thriller [was he thinking of the same film?] and the attempt only
half-worked'. Anne Billson discovered 'none of the self-deprecating
humour of *Commando*, just mindless violence' and decided it was all
'surrogate Norris . . . the only territory [Arnold] is expanding into
is the strictly limited one of Chuck Norris, playing the straight, in-
corruptible hero whose gun-toting antics are never compromised
by a moment's self-doubt.'

There are many opportunities in *Raw Deal* for Arnold's tailor to
show his stuff, as his client parades one expensive suit after another,
even if it looks as if the hangers were still in place. Arnold's performance throughout is strangely lifeless, suggesting that as an
actor he is as stiff as the material on his back, but, given the material
at his disposal, this is not altogether a surprise. Throughout, the
male characters are dull. As for the women, Kaminski's wife has one
brief scene at the beginning and does not reappear, while Kathryn
Harrold makes an unappealing heroine. The ghastly score and the
general air of witlessness that prevails contributes to the view that
nobody's heart or mind was very much engaged in the making of
Raw Deal.

9 Working with Ideas

Predator remains one of Arnold's most fascinating works, better than it first appears, but ultimately not as good as it might have been. In it we detect indecision as to exactly what sort of film it was supposed to be, and what kind of actor Arnold means to present himself as. In a piece that begins by looking like *Star Wars*, quickly moves into a Rambo-like frame of mind, moves slowly into the realms of science fantasy and reverts at its close, all gears crashing, back into Rambo shoot-out mentality, the confusion is not surprising.

For Arnold, however, *Predator* presented a new challenge. 'It is hard work, but I like it because it is fast and full of action . . . it's something a little different for me. I am part of a team. Sure, I am the leader, but the other guys all do something important I can't do. It was one of the reasons I took the script. I like to be part of a team.'

Nevertheless, with *Predator*, as with so many other of his movies, Arnold's considerable good work often went unnoticed by his critics. The crucially percipient *Motion Picture Annual* shrugged off the film by warning its readers to 'never look to Schwarzenegger for any kind of film that doesn't muscle its way through impossible odds, absurd characters, and pygmy-brained scripts.'

The Schwarzenegger physique was obviously important in getting Arnold his latest part, and Arnold worked to keep his body at its peak by a daily hour-long workout in his private gym set up in the ballroom of his hotel in Puetro Vallarta, but in *Predator* his body is used as a symbol for human strength against the strength of things that are inhuman, unworldly and inexplicable, a theme used in *The Terminator* to altogether different effect. Other cast members shared this training time with Arnold, enhancing what was already a team effort. 'It's the best thing that happened to us,' said Bill Duke, one of Arnold's co-stars. 'Working out together helped to bond us. We became so close that we still want to have dinner at night.'

While there may have been an emphasis on *Predator* being a team effort, there was the unalterable truth of a plot that recalled Agatha Christie's *Ten Little Niggers*, gradually eliminating all the supporting cast, and leaving Arnold as the undisputed star of the last part of the movie (rather as Sigourney Weaver is left to dominate *Alien* as her team of players succumb to the inevitable horrors around them). To make all this work, a highly capable production team was assembled.

The director, John McTiernan, was not a well-known name, but quickly proved his ability here and subsequently with *Die Hard* (1988) and *The Hunt for Red October* (1990); Alan Silvestri composed a score, heavily dependent on inventive percussion, that carried the movie forward brilliantly; Donald McAlpine photographed the film with some wonderfully atmospheric results; R. Greenberg contributed superb special effects; and the ultimately physical manifestation of the predator was created by Stan Winston, who had been responsible for the Terminator, and who now brought to the screen a monster reminding at least a few veteran filmgoers of the marvellously ghastly beast in the underrated British *Night of the Demon* (1957). Added to these technicians was a band of seasoned players used to handing in rugged, manly performances, among them Jesse Ventura, who would go on to accompany Arnold into his next movie, Bill Duke and Sylvester Stallone's old boxing adversary from the Rocky series, Carl Weathers; Elpidia Carrillo got a look in as the token female lead.

The opening moments looked familiar. Dutch (Arnold) and his rescue team have been called in by the government to rescue a cabinet minister who has fallen into guerrilla hands in an unfriendly jungle. Dillon (Weathers) gives Dutch his instructions: this is to be a one-day operation, after which the team will be lifted out. Handling such a situation looks easily within the grasp of this seriously macho bunch of warriors, led by Dutch who, with his shades, fat cigar and unshaven face, is the essence of laid-back.

Once in the jungle, things quickly appear to be very different from what Dillon has led Dutch to believe. The men discover the hanging bodies of three of their colleagues, Green Berets who have been skinned alive. Now we not only see the men moving through the inhospitable country, but watch them through the eyes of some other being, as moving shapes seen with infra-red sensitivity. When the men come across the camp where the hostages are supposedly being held, an orgiastic shoot-out erupts.

Dutch refuses to participate further in the set-up. 'My men are not expendable,' he tells Dillon, 'and I don't do this sort of work.' Anna (Carrillo) is taken by the men on their journey across the border to be picked up. One of the men crushes a scorpion. Through the eyes of the 'thing' we have already seen a scorpion-like shape being nurtured in the hand of the monster. Soon, according to Anna, the jungle is 'coming alive' and taking the men. Blood and hideous details remain, but the bodies disappear. The inevitable occurs to the men: 'We're all gonna die.'

Dutch and the team attempt to outwit the unknown enemy, laying traps and trip wires to ensnare it, to no avail. Anna explains that this phenomenon is not unknown to her people; in the hottest years they have sometimes found the skinned remains of their men; old women have crossed themselves in an effort to ward off the supernatural evil among them. Mac is almost demented in his quest of the enemy, locates it, but is killed. Billy, too, is driven to almost sacrificial feats by the presence of the unknown. He presents himself to the open sky, slashes his chest with a knife for the beast to be drawn by his blood, and waits. He dies, as does Dillon and the rest of the team.

Now there is only the elemental confrontation between the predator and Dutch. Pursued by his enemy, Dutch crashes into the jungle's torrents, and manages to clamber to land where the predator is still pursuing him. Dutch realizes the predator cannot see him when he is encased in mud and, at full moon, lights a flare and lets out a wild animal cry, alerting the predator to attend in its all too solid state. Stumbling into a lake, the protecting mud is washed from Dutch. The predator pinions his adversary and unmasks his full horror, unleashing a maelstrom of Stan Winston's startling effects.

Dutch may be forgiven his reaction, 'What the hell are you?', which seems to be the extent of his scientific interest in the beast (Dutch, after all, is hardly a Professor Challenger). Apparently amused to be able to commit suicide, the predator taps some keys and self-destructs in a mega-explosion. Dutch is rescued by the helicopter which happily contains Anna, but is clearly traumatized by his experience. He will, we assume, be a sadder but wiser man, another reason for us to link him up with Rambo in one of his more contemplative, post-chaos states.

Opening in the USA on 12 June 1987, *Predator* took some $34 million in its first three weeks, with Arnold's reputation boosted by his director, who claimed he could well be the new John Wayne. The critics reaction to the movie was mixed. Quentin Falk thought it 'dazzling to look at, but distasteful to contemplate too deeply'. Roger Ebert wrote that 'This is the kind of idea that is produced at the end of a ten-second brainstorming session, but if it's done well, who cares?'

More intelligent than *Commando* and *Raw Deal*, *Predator* shows its star's fondness for the science fiction-fantasy genre, one that he is able to dominate (as *The Terminator* had shown) as much by a presence as by a giant role. True, *Predator* has its fair share of shoot-outs and multiple explosions, and the bloodiness of the various deaths yield nothing to any other Schwarzenegger movies, but here Arnold is given considerable time and space to hand in a proper acting performance.

He manages it, rising to the challenge of being the only actor around (except for the long-suffering Kevin Peter Hall manipulating the Predator) for the last twenty minutes or so. What is so important is that here, even stronger than earlier in the picture, John Vallone's superb artwork – now responsible for the gloriously artificial jungle scenes – provides a background that is a feast for the senses. In these last sequences of elemental conflict between man and the unknown, we could want no finer example of cunning brawn than Arnold. His kill-first-and-ask-questions-later philosophy may not be intellectually endearing, but in the circumstances is

Arnold Schwarzenegger, American citizen, born Thal, Austria, July 30 1947 – probably the most potent presence to dominate international cinema throughout the 1980s

Not intended as a tribute to Arnold's heroes Steve Reeves or Reg Park, the much retitled *Hercules Goes Bananas* was a cockeyed attempt to introduce picturegoers to a muscleman by the name of Arnold Strong

Arnold in the mid-seventies seems intent on building muscle, but delivers his first proper acting performance in the quirky *Stay Hungry* opposite Jeff Bridges

(Above) Taking a rest from *Pumping Iron* with an upside down Franco Columbu and admiring attendants. (Below) Already contemplating a career beyond bodybuilding at the time of *Pumping Iron*

The Barbie doll-like Ann Margret, the desperately mugging Kirk Douglas and the crisply turned out Arnold as the naïve hero of the ill-fated Western spoof *The Villain*

Unwilling or unable to read the words on the card, Arnold as Conan the Barbarian contemplates a future as the muscle-bound star of lavish prehistoric epics written and directed by John Milius

Grace Jones' gauntness strikingly complements Arnold's muscular meanness during a serious moment of *Conan the Destroyer*, a mildly effective and workmanlike sequel

The Terminator successfully portrayed Arnold as a villain of an almost Frankenstein's monster-like indestructibility; it also helped to diminish the appeal of Sylvester Stallone, which beside that of Schwarzenegger, seemed so vulnerable

A half-hearted try at establishing Brigitte Nielsen as something more than a shapely starlet, *Red Sonja* pushed Arnold into second place, and proved the redundancy of his Conan image in the mid-eighties

Sometimes softly sentimental, sometimes sickeningly violent, *Commando* set Arnold's unquestionable decency against the sado-masochism of a chain-mailed and leathered nasty played by Vernon Wells

Guns, so often the symbol of might employed in Arnold's films (as here in *Raw Deal*), seemed little more than expected, fashionable trinkets in 1986. By 1993, Arnold's attitude to them had apparently changed

(Above) *Predator* showed its star (seen here with Carl Weathers) to good advantage, evidence that his movies were of a higher quality than critics sometimes allowed. (Below) *The Running Man*'s satire on the evils of television was an Orwellian nightmare that offered Richard Dawson (centre) as the hateful games show host more acting opportunities than the quilted Arnold

eminently practical.

Perhaps, too, we recognize in Arnold an innate intelligence which he is able to communicate on screen, though it is clearly harder to spot it in some films than in others. In the straightforward all-action pictures, we need not look for such intelligence, and don't expect to find it (though it is often there) but in Arnold's science fiction he is in every way in control of the proceedings. Almost always, too, his science-fiction movies have attracted better writers, and cinema-goers remember quality. Arnold has proved skilful in selecting properties that exploit the natural qualities he can bring to this type of film.

A naïve actor might have blanched at the role of *The Terminator*, with its few lines of dialogue, its totally unsympathetic character, and the fact that it vanishes towards the end of the film. Arnold saw its possibilities, and the quality of the work happening around it. If his next movie was another attempt to establish himself as a master of the science-fiction movie, it almost certainly did him no harm.

As big an event as *Predator* was Arnold's marriage to Maria, on 26 April 1986, which attracted massive media interest. The importance of the day had been underlined by the guest list Arnold and Maria had drawn up, which included Ronald Reagan, Pope John Paul II and Kurt Waldheim. None of the three got there, but the invitation to Waldheim was one that Arnold probably regretted having made when Waldheim's integrity as a world leader was blown sky high with allegations of involvement with the Nazis. Arnold was careful to point out that he had only met Waldheim on one previous occasion, after a call from Waldheim's office had proposed a meeting. Though unable to attend the ceremony, Waldheim at least made sure he would be remembered by sending the newly-weds a papier mâché sculpture that had Arnold, in lederhosen, attempting to ravish a doll-like Maria, suitably turned out in dirndl.

Waldheim's gift may have seemed in dubious taste, but the day, with Franco Columbu as best man, passed off as extravagantly and successfully as planned. While some in Hollywood doubtless waited for the first cracks to appear in the new marriage, Maria (whose career had taken a leap ahead when she was named anchor person for the high-profile CBS Morning News) and Arnold began a married life that has so far survived without a hint of discord.

'Stallone? He's not competing with my movies; he's doing his own stuff and I do mine,' said Arnold around the time of *The Running Man*. In truth, by 1987 Stallone was having to compete with his own Rocky and Rambo movies as much as with anything Arnold was up to. Stallone had followed up *Rambo: First Blood Part II* (good) with *Rocky IV* (laboured) and *Cobra* (weak), and in 1986 failed convincingly to soften his image with *Over the Top* (flaccid).

As for Arnold, since the heady excellence of *The Terminator* he had turned out some reasonable, some dodo, movies, but seemed in general to be surer-footed than his old rival. Now, with *The Running Man*, it was back to science-fiction with a film that had seemed destined never to get to the screen.

Based on Richard Bachman's (Stephen King's) novel, the screenplay by Steven E. de Souza (who had also written *Commando*) suffered a long run of bad luck. Christopher Reeve had been mooted as the original star when plans were announced for George Pan Cosmatos (already responsible for *First Blood* and *Cobra*) to direct in 1985, but it was not to be. When Cosmatos promised that his budget would zoom to something like $18 million, the producers waved him goodbye – perhaps unjustly, as the ultimate budget came in around $27 million. With Reeve also out of the picture, and Arnold in, another director, Carl Schenkel, whose 1984 West German *Out of Order* had showed he could further tense a good script, appeared on the scene. Whatever Schenkel's qualities, they were not right for *The Running Man*, and he hurriedly vanished.

Ferdinand Fairfax was given to understand he was directing the film, but quickly moved aside so that Andrew Davis could take his place. Davis actually put one or two scenes in the can, but after a few days he too fell by the directorial wayside. It was now time for Paul Michael Glaser, Starsky from TV's cult *Starsky and Hutch*, to move in – and stay. The fact that he had only one other directing credit – *Band of the Hand* (1986), a dimly appreciated effort about the effect of a Vietnam veteran on a set of juvenile delinquents in Miami – didn't seem to worry the producers, who by this stage were fairly desperate to have any sort of name taking responsibility for shooting the movie.

Pulled in at the last minute, with a mere two days to gather himself before he began work, it was clear that Glaser would have a limited effect on the way the movie turned out. If it became largely a matter of pointing the camera at the right person at the right time, Glaser at least helped inject a sense of style and flavour. What he couldn't do was overturn de Souza's screenplay, which suffered from an ability to pass itself off as several other, and better, movie scripts; everything in *The Running Man* is a reminder of something similar done elsewhere. Some of this may be Stephen King's fault, for de Souza pretty well sticks to King's scenario, while substituting Arnold's triumphantly happy ending for King's tragic finale with our dying hero piloting a plane, kamikaze-like, into the TV Games Building.

In a futuristic, blatantly Orwellian world, the decent and conscientious government pilot Ben Richards (Arnold) refuses to fire on unarmed civilians involved in a food riot. Put to hard labour for his refusal to toe the vicious official line, he breaks out and links up with the resistance movement. He meets up with attractive conformist Amber Mendez (Maria Conchita Alonso) and uses her to help him escape the country, but she shops him to the airport authorities, and he is despatched to Damon Killian (Richard Dawson), the producer-presenter of the vastly successful TV game-show *The Running Man*.

Here is a society where TV assumes a terrifying importance, where propaganda and prizes ('earn a double bonus for reporting a family member') dominate in a culture that has been brainwashed into subservience. In subjecting criminals and the totally innocent fall-guys of the government to the horrors of *The Running Man*, where death at the hands of the Stalkers (quirky, merciless and government-sponsored executioners who hunt down the stars of the game-show) is the inevitable, and only, prize, Killian provides a safety-valve for the collected suppressed violence of the masses.

Richards, promoted by Killian as 'The Butcher of Bakersfield', is a much harder nut to crack than our game-host is used to. In a series of devastating encounters with the various Stalkers, Richards' fellow-escapees perish, but Mendez – propelled by the ratings-

conscious Killian into the maelstrom of the show – lives through to
the closing credits. The odious Killian wheedles and oils his way to
the denouement, where his welcome come-uppance is to die in his
own brief participation, arranged for the cameras by Richards himself, in the killing entertainment.

Half the fun of watching this movie is notching up the others
that it recalls – *1984* and *Brazil* (the ascendancy of the state over the
individual; the omnipotence of an unknown Big Brother), *Roller-
ball, Death Race 2000* and others (the manipulation of violence in
sport to maintain the contentment of a social status quo). The one
full-scale city landscape we catch a glimpse of is so obviously a
painting with a model train moving gingerly across it that we think
lovingly back to the bewitching model railway station cheekily used
for the opening credits of Hitchcock's *The Lady Vanishes*. The
heroine of *The Running Man* who, having handed over the innocent
hero to the baddies, thinking them goodies, realizes her error and
does what she can to right it, has her precursor in Madeleine Carroll's heroine of *The 39 Steps* (Hitchcock again). *The Running Man*'s
'winners', supposedly enjoying the *dolce vita* on some exotic beach,
but who have met a very different fate, take us back to a well-
remembered scene in the patchy *Capricorn One*.

Meanwhile, the scenes set in Killian's TV studios recall almost
every parody of that industry that has appeared, with Killian himself often reminding us of Peter Sellers' marvellously insincere TV
games-host in the 1957 *The Naked Truth*.

If these constant filmic reminders take our attention from the
plot, the Stalkers themselves, deadly as they are, are meant to make
us laugh. Some of them succeed. Dynamo is a vast, lumbering blob
of fat lit up like a Christmas tree, shooting off volts while firing off
sub-Handelian castrato arias. He is a diverting curiosity, though it
is chastening to know the actor playing him died just a few weeks
after shooting wound up. It seemed almost inevitable to Arnold:
'The heart was not meant to pump blood through a body like that.'

There is also the simperingly-smiled Subzero (played by Professor Toru Tanaka), and the genuinely funny Jesse Ventura as the
put-upon muscular Captain Freedom. They all look like absurdities
on loan from World Championship Wrestling. Other touches go to

make this film as funny as it is exciting, including some delicious characterization of Killian's besotted audience, blinded by its own lust for primeval justice and its overwhelming admiration of its front-man. In fact, Dawson is the linchpin of this film, turning in a performance of accurate unattractiveness that is a joy to see. This is an inspired piece of casting fully grasped by Dawson, his talents honed by his years as the real-life host of a hugely popular American game-show, *Family Feud*.

It was Dawson who received most of what praise was handed out when the movie appeared. Julian Petley in the *Monthly Film Bulletin* found 'a certain heavy-handedness in scenes relying on dialogue or humour . . . The film ends up facing both ways at once by providing exactly the same kind of violence spectacle that it criticizes Killian for manufacturing, and twenty-first-century audiences for watching.' Vincent Canby decided it 'has the manners and the gadgetry of a sci-fi adventure, but is, at heart, an engagingly mean, cruel, nasty, funny send-up of television', while the ever-perceptive *Motion Picture Annual* thought that 'Dawson contributes an intelligence and depth here not provided by the screenplay or the director, and makes this film his exclusive property'. Turning to the film's star, Stephen Dark for the *Virgin Film Yearbook* noted an 'uneasy marriage between Neanderthal strength and Austrian deadpan humour in a poorly-delineated futuristic setting'. Brian Case had difficulty in taking any of it very seriously: 'Big Arnie's quilted outfit makes him look like a duvet.'

10   Comic Elements

Arnold's next movie was probably the best piece of work he had done since The *Terminator*, and more entertaining than most of his career to date. Arnold signed up for $10 million, happy that his director was Walter Hill, whose track record as writer, producer and director was impressive. Along the way, Hill had produced *Alien* (1979), been story-writer and executive producer for *Aliens* (1986), and scored a directorial and co-writing hit with *48 Hrs* (1982), where Eddie Murphy and Nick Nolte battled personalities and street crime in an archetypal buddy movie.

In *Red Heat*, everything seems to have come together to make a thoroughly professional, entertaining picture. If the movie had been made thirty or forty years earlier in black and white and without the strong language, it might have made a very good *film noir*. It has style, wit and an arrow-sharp determination to do what it sets out to do; like all good *films noir*, it also looks impressive.

Hill is supposed to have told Arnold, 'I want you for a movie in which you'll be recreating a Greta Garbo part.' Having heard of *Tootsie*, Arnold wondered if Hill had a drag role lined up for him until Hill whispered the title *Ninotchka* and explained that, like Garbo in an earlier age, Arnold's character would be a Russian travelling to a foreign country.

This time around the route was from Russia to Chicago, the character Captain Ivan Danko, a no-nonsense, humourless, straight-down-the-line Russian soldier. The Russianness was important, and Arnold had vocal training for the Russian dialogue scenes, and the will to lose the ten pounds Hill asked him to shed in the pursuit of looking more convincingly Slav. Since this was a project Arnold believed in (and it shows on screen) he was happy to comply, artfully realizing that Hill's concept was in tune with current perceptions about US-Russian relations. 'I loved this idea,' said Arnold. 'It fitted the new climate you could see if you read the papers.'

At the same time, Stallone was putting himself through several kinds of hell making *Rambo III*, which would show up as a crass misunderstanding of how the world, and the cinema audience, was reading world politics. Whereas Stallone's Russians were as black as any melodramatic villain had ever been, Arnold's Russians were very, very Russian, and never presented as the enemy, just as different.

The clash of cultures, indeed, throws up many of the film's best moments in a screenplay (Hill, Harry Kleiner, and a writer mostly remembered in Britain for his *Z Cars* scripts, Troy Kennedy Martin) that seldom misses its mark. As violent as most other Schwarzenegger movies, *Red Heat* nevertheless retains a sort of innocence for much of its highly energetic span, not least because Arnold's opening punches must be the kerpows on which the fisticuffs of Batman were based. Punching has never sounded so artificial as in Hill's opening scene, but this is how punching should sound, and this is one of Hill's little specialities, reinventing the sound by whacking a leather sofa with a ping-pong bat.

The authentic feel of the picture is helped by the scenes shot in Budapest and Moscow, where the authorities gave Hill permission to film in Red Square, the first time an American film company had been allowed to do so. The path to such permission may have been made easier by the fact that Arnold was well known in the USSR through his work with the Bodybuilding Federation of the Soviet Union. Not too much can be made of the Red Square location (the most obvious moment comes at the end of the movie when Arnold stands looking directly at us, beamingly proud as the credits roll), but the sense of place that pervades the Russian scenes at the start of the movie is so strong we can almost smell it.

It is at times like this that we notice the quality of work Arnold is now involved in (James Horner's score, *Boris Godunov*-like with its clamouring bells and intoning choir; John Vallone's flavoursome evocation of a back street Russian café), and to which he responds admirably. *Red Heat* also provides Arnold with a brief return home for the shooting of the snow-fight scene in Schladming, near Graz, but what should have been a good experience was marred by the death of his friend, the second unit director and stunt co-ordinator Bennie Dobbins, whose collapse and death from a heart attack in February 1988 deeply affected Arnold. His cancelled appearance at the Vienna Opera Ball with Maria was only one mark of the deep respect he had for his colleague.

This is also the first movie in which Arnold, perhaps responding to a fashion, lines himself up with a second leading man who is more or less on a level with him (*Twins* would be the next, and most impressive, example of this tendency). Contrast is important in the pairing of all leads of buddy movies, but possibly even more so with Arnold. At least his unique qualities make such a co-lead easier to discover. In *Red Heat*, the job fell to James Belushi, whose slightly stodgy but appealing openness had come over in such films as Michael Mann's *Thief* (1981) and Oliver Stone's *Salvador* (1986). Belushi exuded the streetwise weariness of what we like to think of as Chicago cops, with the air of steadily going to seed that made him a perfect foil to Arnold's supreme physicality.

The two men liked working with each other, and it is a relationship that clicks on screen, even if it reminds us of other heroes and sidekicks, not least Stallone's shade-wearing policeman and his junk-eating Sancho Panza in the generally regrettable *Cobra* (1986). The difference is that in Hill's piece the star makes room for his co-stars, and has insisted on good situations and dialogue. Even the Russian (or Soviet, as Danko is careful to distinguish) villain, effectively snarled by the unlikely Ed O'Ross, comes across well, despite not having much conversation or depth.

We see many nude male bodies, pumping their iron and staring suspiciously out of the mist of a steam bath, before Arnold, his body the last to arrive at the ball, appears, bare-assed and covered only by a tenuous little Greek covering. The image, as so often with the first image we have of Arnold in his films, is memorable.

Arnold, Captain Danko, is after Viktor Rostavili, a murdering drug-smuggler whose criminal brother Danko has already killed in the pursuit of his duties. After a preliminary scrap in the deep snows around the steam house (these persistent contrasts of heat and ice work well) Danko is directed to a café where Viktor may be found. Viktor is there, but escapes after killing Danko's friend and colleague, and makes his way, with two accomplices, to Chicago, where he is apprehended for going through a red light. The Russians know he has been organizing a huge drug delivery to the Soviet Union. and charge Danko with travelling to Chicago to bring him back, without letting the American police know why.

In Chicago Danko is awarded a disillusioned, trouble-prone cop with a serious attitude problem, Art Ridzik (Belushi), to look after him. Danko is unimpressed with what he sees of the West, insisting on staying in the seedy joint where Viktor was arrested. He switches on the TV to find a porn movie grinding away. 'Capitalism,' he sighs. At police headquarters Ridzik's boss gives a comprehensive account of how men in the West avoid stress. Asked for his own method, Danko replies 'Vodka.'

Danko captures Viktor, but is ambushed, and Viktor again escapes, though Danko manages to grasp a key that is in Viktor's possession. A disgraced Danko is told by officials from his mother country to return to Russia, and decides to go undercover; he knows the key will eventually lead him to Viktor. Ridzik is denounced by his understanding superiors as 'a total expert at fucking-up'.

It becomes clear that Danko and Ridzik are sought by the well-disciplined organization, almost a cult (whose every member must shave his head in obedience), through which Viktor is dealing in cocaine. After speaking to Viktor's wife Catherine (Gina Gershon), Danko and Ridzik are waylaid by the gang, and Viktor tells Danko he wants the key. Ridzik has put one of Viktor's two accomplices in hospital, and takes Danko to visit him there in the hope of learning more. Before the patient can talk, his compatriot, disguised as a nurse, gives him a lethal injection. Showing a softer side, Danko lets Catherine, who is innocent, escape. He bonds closer with Ridzik, though there are areas of American culture he does not understand ('Who is Dirty Harry?' he asks).

Catherine phones Danko at his hotel to tell him the big deal is about to take place, and she wants out. Viktor and his men arrive at

Danko's hotel. Viktor rescues his key and means to shoot Danko, but has to make a quick dive into a convenient river. Catherine is found with her neck broken. Tired of it all, the police bosses pull Danko and Ridzik off the case, but Arnold traces the number of the key, which he has recorded, to the type used at the bus terminal. It is here that Viktor completes the hand-over, only to find himself confronted by Danko.

Ridzik, fearing Danko will kill Viktor, demands that he should be the one to take him in, but the argument becomes academic when Viktor gets away and commandeers a bus. Danko climbs aboard another, joined by Ridzik, and pursues him through an impressive chase across town ('That was a fucking Chicago landmark,' complains Ridzik at one point). Finally, the two buses stand face to face, as Danko and Viktor prepare to obliterate each other. At the last moment, Ridzik gets control of Danko's steering wheel and averts the head-to-head collision, but Viktor meets an oncoming railway locomotive. He survives even this, however, and Ridzik can do little but bow out ('I give up. This whole thing's very Russian'). Danko kills Viktor. As Danko prepares to return to the USSR, he tells Ridzik it is possible for them to like one another; they are policemen, not politicians.

The opportunity presented by *Red Heat* to hand in a proper performance is seized by Arnold, who makes Danko likeable and believable. His responses to Belushi's fruity playing (sometimes with the disadvantage of dialogue that sounds sloppily extempore) are genuinely funny, pushing Arnold's talent as a comic actor fast forward. When, in the closing moments, we see Danko's obvious fondness for Ridzik for the first time – a very clever sequence, for we notice that Ridzik is unaware of it – Hill does not encourage the movie into mawkishness; the playing remains level-headed and strong.

Much of the movie is derivative, and some of the reminders seem very near to home, and from the movies of Sylvester Stallone. Catherine's scenes in dance class and the subsequent car park scene hark back to Brigitte Nielsen's appearances in *Cobra*, while the final concentrated conflict between Danko's bus and Viktor's bus has an exactly equivalent scene as the denouement of *Rambo III*. *Red Heat* may have many qualities, but its reception at the box-office was not overwhelming. The cost had turned out around $30 million, and only $16 million found its way back into the backers' pockets.

Plans to make *Twins*, Arnold's first true comedy, went back as far as 1985; five years later, and it would almost certainly not have been so difficult to get off the ground. By the time it hit the screens, Arnold's enthusiasm was obvious: 'I've wanted to do this kind of film, a comedy, for a long time . . . The good thing about making this film is that none of us needed immediate money. So we were able to go to the studio and say, "Hey, let's make this film for $15 million, and we won't take any salary." That made it cheap, right?'

No salary, perhaps, but this did not mean no money. Costing $18 million, *Twins* ultimately took over $110 million in the USA alone, from which Arnold had contracted to take a sizeable 17.5% of any profits. The deal was put together with the head of Universal, Tom Pollock, with the two stars, Arnold and the diminutive Danny De-Vito, and director Ivan Reitman, all working for no fee but taking a slice of the profits. As Pollock pointed out this arrangement seemed to represent a gamble, but if the gamble paid off (and they were pretty confident it would) the parties involved knew they would probably be making a very great deal more money out of it than if they had signed a conventional contract.

Perhaps the publicity campaign's most amusing idea said everything that needed to be said about *Twins*; huge posters of Danny DeVito appeared bearing the legend Schwarzenegger, and posters of Schwarzenegger appeared bearing the legend DeVito. In its sheer unlikeliness, there was a potency in the pairing of the two actors, though this accentuated the fact that the film was really a one-joke piece. The success of the movie depended on the mileage that could be got out of that one joke, and Ivan Reitman, of all the directors available and queuing up for the privilege of working with Arnold, seemed most likely to succeed in bringing it off. Born in Czechoslovakia in 1946, Reitman had spent most of his childhood in Canada, and by the early 1970s had embarked on a film career as an editor, composer, producer and director, reaching a sort of apogee with the hugely profitable *Ghostbusters* (1984).

One of the main problems facing Reitman when shooting began in New Mexico in the spring of 1988 was the reinvention of Arnold as a comic actor, relying on a thick coating of practised charm which would transform Arnold into a giant Chaplinesque figure. Here at last was Arnold the innocent, still standing at the door of adult understanding and disillusion. To some this was a hard pill to swallow, and there is a lurking suspicion that the niceness of Arnold's persona in this movie is so manipulated as to verge on the absurd, especially when seen alongside the mean aggressiveness and urban know-how of DeVito.

It is no slight that Vincent Benedict (DeVito) refers to Julius Benedict (Arnold), a little way into the movie, as 'a 230 pound virgin'; though DeVito makes this a very funny aside, why should the weight of a virgin accentuate the virgin's comedic potential? We know from the beginning of the movie that our two heroes, utterly dissimilar physically as they may be, are indeed twins, the result of a Nazi-like plot to produce a perfect specimen from the sperm of six fathers, carefully selected for their very special and shining qualities. Julius was consequently born to the chosen mother, followed a few minutes later, and most unexpectedly, by his twin brother Vincent. Mother Nature's unfair trick on the experiment was to give Julius the exemplary and finest characteristics of his fathers, and then stand by as 'all the crap' from the fathers went into his twin brother. Separated at birth, the two men grow up in ignorance of each other, believing their mother to have died or deserted them in infanthood.

When Julius learns that he is a twin, he travels to America to find his brother and with him find their mother. Undaunted by the fact that Vincent is a seedy, totally disreputable and faithless small-time con-man, who merely uses Julius' interest to get him out of jail, Julius clings to his belief in his quest, and Vincent slowly comes to realize the truth and importance of what is happening. The brothers sport and fall in love (Arnold's first attempt at anything like an everyday love scene) and Vincent, inevitably, gets enmeshed in the biggest crime of his life, way out of his depth. If there was any doubt of his devotion, Julius arrives to rescue him from death at the hands of his assassin.

Meanwhile their respective girlfriends accompany the twins as they try to find their mother. They visit a foundation where an elderly lady tells them their mother is there in spirit only; she is dead. Rescued from his twilit, seedy world of crime, Vincent has found a new happiness and confidence in his relationship with Julius. Their happiness is made complete when their mother (the lady who had told them she was dead) welcomes them into her open arms. Our last glimpse of the brothers is with their wives, wheeling out perambulators in which two sets of new twins give us the film's final *coup de grâce*.

Opening in the USA on 5 December 1988, *Twins* was generally given a warm welcome (it was a warm movie), with critics appreciating the new charms Arnold brought to the picture. Roger Ebert, while noticing the fact that Arnold handled the comedy scenes with ease, felt that *Twins* was 'not a great comedy ... but it is an engaging entertainment with some big laughs and a sort of warm goofiness'. In the *Monthly Film Bulletin*, Anne Billson couldn't praise Reitman's handling of the material, pointing out that 'it is left to the two leads to inject some pizzazz into the proceedings, which they manage to do with admirable professionalism and charm'.

The professionalism and charm was clearly not in evidence when journalist Christena Appleyard talked to Arnold around the time of *Twins*. She found 'an odd man. Detached, chilly, obsessive. He walks and talks with an exaggerated slowness that convinces you he is full of secrets. Listening to him "open up" about his personal feelings is like sitting next to a fridge with the door open.' This Arnold sounds a very different man from the one he portrays in *Twins*.

Whatever the truth about Arnold's true personality (and it is not given to any except those closest to him to fully understand what that may be), it does not get in the way of his convincing us of his character on screen. The trick of *Twins* is to a great extent the trick of Arnold; it has little to do with great acting or a great script. We can see that DeVito is a remarkable actor with a wonderful gift for physical comedy of a type that Arnold could never hope to achieve. Perhaps Arnold's true contribution to this movie is to be cast against type, but the degree to which Arnold brings this off is in itself pretty remarkable; the fact that it is so knowing an achievement does not make it any less effective or charming. When Arnold passes a billboard of Stallone as John Rambo, looks up at it, grins and passes by, it is not only Julius wondering at the absurdity of such macho grandeur in the sophisticated world beyond the backwaters he has grown up in, but Arnold pointing out that while Stallone might be content to be forever identified (and forever trapped) as a symbol of indomitable strength, Arnold was not. The ability to play the chameleon was fast becoming one of Arnold's most expected characteristics.

11 All in the Mind

As we have seen, what Sylvester Stallone was up to mattered a great deal to Arnold. 1990, the year of *Total Recall*, showed Arnold, and any others who cared to investigate, quite clearly who was winning the race, and why.

While Stallone had been locked into Rocky and Rambo movies, Rocky winding up alongside *Total Recall* as the 1990 *Rocky V*, Arnold had been not only solidifying his reputation for muscle-bound all-action movies, but had made conscious efforts to surround himself with good writers, good directors and good ideas. As Stallone lurched from one misconceived box-office clinker to another (and it didn't matter that he gave appealing performances in several of them), Arnold succeeded in every field in which Stallone had tried and failed. Stallone had gone for comedy in *Rhinestone* (1984), but who remembers this against Arnold's comedy debut in the vastly superior *Twins* (1988)?

Science fiction has also provided Arnold with a genre totally unexplored by Stallone, a genre that reached its peak with *Total Recall*. And Arnold has never allowed himself to be too closely identified with one character. He escaped De Laurentiis' clutches and the Conan character after three increasingly feeble movies and, although he played the Terminator twice, between 1984 and 1991 he had turned from being a bad Terminator to a good one.

This masterly stroke speaks volumes about Arnold's power to retain an immediate identification with his audience while yet insisting on his own, new contribution to the work in hand. It may seem unfair ever to expect Rocky to switch from good to bad, or for Rambo to start working for whichever government represents the

currently fashionable 'other side', for both Rocky and Rambo are
flesh-and-blood characters, bounded by culture, whereas the Terminator, when all is said and done, is no more than a machine. We
then have to consider Arnold's achievement in making us feel that
machines can be both good and bad.

Arnold's director for *Total Recall* was 51-year-old Paul Verhoeven; for Arnold, the only choice when De Laurentiis went out of
business and there was once again the possibility of making the
movie. 'As soon as I heard I jumped on it again. I called Carolco and
said buy it immediately, today, this evening when I call back, you
have to have it. And that's exactly what happened. The next day I
met Paul Verhoeven. I've met him several times before. I wanted to
work with him for a long time . . . He read it and I said let's make a
deal immediately.'

Verhoeven had worked his way into international movies
through an apprenticeship as a maker of documentaries for the
Royal Dutch Navy and several home-grown TV series. Several of
his early works showed his predilection for using Rutger Hauer as
his leading man, as in his first film to prove he could direct an
exportable success, *Turkish Delight* (1973), an erotic account of a
marriage between Hauer and his co-star Monique Van de Ven.
Never a prolific director (in the 1980s he made only four films), his
work was almost always worth waiting for, his reputation growing
from the 1979 World War II picture *Soldier of Orange*, through
Flesh and Blood (1985), an American-Dutch movie about the
Middle Ages, to *Robocop* (1987). *Total Recall* was Verhoeven's first
movie in three years, and one to which he brought the skill and in-
sight he showed for the science fiction genre in *Robocop*. Such
blatant flair must have appealed to Arnold, who was now expected
to work alongside intelligent, resourceful directors. When Verhoeven spoke about his work, there was no mistaking him for
somebody from the De Laurentiis camp. 'Science fiction for me
always has a philosophical level,' he explained. 'It's a way of
expressing something you can't express otherwise. SF should
always be poetic. It has to do with the divine, and with God, or
other levels of paradise, or other worlds that you want to believe in.'

In the case of *Total Recall*, it also had to do with Philip K. Dick.

Hollywood had had his short story 'We Can Remember It For You Wholesale' in mind for some years. As far back as the mid-seventies, Ronald Shusett had ambitions to film the work, which was acquired by the Walt Disney organization, which would have made who knows what of the author's exhilarating ideas.

Somewhere along the way, the ubiquitous Dino De Laurentiis intended to make a movie of it, acquiring the property in 1982. De Laurentiis originally fancied Richard Dreyfuss as his leading man; by the time he got around to considering Arnold he had decided on a director who didn't come up to Arnold's expectations, David Cronenburg. Arnold declined to sign. In 1986, a new director, Bruce Beresford, was brought in, to make the movie in Australia with up-and-coming Patrick Swayze. But the De Laurentiis movie empire was in trouble, and with the collapse of its business portfolio, including the already $6 million wasted on the Dick film, it looked as if Dick's fascinating story would never reach the screen. The screenplay ended up as the topic for favourite discussion at the American Film Institute as one of the great unproduced films of Hollywood. It was largely through Arnold's determination that this failure began turning to success.

'I was instrumental in getting some of the missing elements together,' he said modestly. 'And because of my positive outlook I can be helpful. I'm always there to pull things together, pour a thimbleful of schnapps, put on the Austrian music, cheer things up and keep everything on track.'

The strong base on which the success of *Total Recall* would be built, Dick's story, cannot be overestimated – all along the line those involved in the film's making responded to the quality of his material. Dick's vastly resourceful and often technical approach to his fiction was tempered by some idiosyncratic personal traits. Nine years after writing this particular story Dick's life changed after a shaft of pink light passed supernatural information into him. His body was used in other ways, as when Elijah seemed to occupy his being, or when he felt his body was suddenly in ancient Rome.

For much of his life, clearly, Dick was a troubled man, some of his disturbances possibly rooted in the sexual abuse he had endured as a young boy. Whatever the reasons, adulthood brought its traumas fast on one another's heels, including five marriages (he had a fixation for dark-haired women, which finds its repercussions in the *Total Recall* story), several suicide attempts, and a terror of eating.

It has been suggested that Dick may have been suffering from a disorder known as temporal lobe epilepsy, whose symptoms of intense religious fervour, hallucinations, and the overpowering urge to write certainly seem to match a man we might otherwise charitably call hyperactive. He waited passionately for Christ's second coming, and expected the first sighting of the Messiah to take place in Belgium; an expectancy hinted at by the ending of *Total Recall*. It cannot be denied that his illness, whatever it may have been, gave brilliance to his work, a mass of fiction that deals largely with the blurring of reality, written with an extraordinarily high level of invention. His prose zaps along, sharp, easy, distinctive, convincing, intellectual but always recognizable as an extension of our own lives. When we read Dick we cannot fail to see ourselves in his characters, projected into some future, unknown, dream-like state.

The original story was written in the autumn of 1965, a perfect example of short-story-telling which bears a striking resemblance to the film based upon it. Douglas Quail, a salaried clerk, tires of his mundane existence and cannot stop dreaming of visiting Mars, a constant irritation to his wife Kirsten. A robotic cab-driver takes him to Rekal Incorporated, an organization that offers to implant in his mind the memory of a visit to Mars, complete with mementoes, giving the benefit of the experience without the inconvenience and expense. Quail also elects that he will make this imaginary visit as a secret agent.

The Rekal technicians prepare Quail for treatment but, under sedation, they discover his mind already has a real-life memory of a visit to Mars, where he indeed worked as a secret agent. His knowledge of his time there discomforts the Interplan police, who tell him he must die. Quail argues that he will give himself up to Rekal, allowing the true memory to be wiped clean and a new fantasy, devised by his captors, to be introduced in its place. Quail will then be given artefacts of the experience, which turns out to be an imagined meeting with a race of alien, field-mice-like creatures planning to take over Earth. They have, it seems, given Quail their word that, so long as he lives, they will resist the temptation to attack his planet.

The Rekal boffins are about to introduce this experience to Quail when they discover that their proposed implant already exists as a real-life memory in his brain. As Dick's brief tale snaps shut we realize that Quail will not now be killed, for his death will surely bring about the end of life on Earth.

There is much here that a careful observer of *Total Recall* will recognize. In the film, Quail becomes Quaid; perhaps the possibility of the hero being muddled up with the then current US Vice-President, Dan Quayle, was too awful to contemplate. We are also expected to believe that Quaid is a naturally bright, if ordinary, working man, not the sort of man, as Dan Quayle was, to spell potato with an 'e'. Dick's clerk is transformed into a construction worker, presumably because it looks better to have Arnold pushing a pneumatic drill rather than a pen. We recognize the computerized cab-driver, too, brilliantly brought to wooden life, though his sparse dialogue in the story has a little more edge to it. We do not recognize the alien race of field-mice-like invaders, but the main thrust of Dick's ideas, essential to the well-being of the movie, is intact.

There is a possible warning note in Dick's theory that some ideas simply refuse to turn out as full-length novels; the job Verhoeven and his creative team had on hand was to turn a perfectly-formed short story into a full-length film. The task was formidable. The only studio that could cope with the demands made by the screenplay was the Churubusco Studio in Mexico City, having ten sound stages on which the movie could be built. Mexico provided an inhospitable environment, with poor conditions leading to much sickness among the company. This added to the stress endemic to such a vast project, presided over by the sometimes explosive Verhoeven.

Film clearly demands an opening out of the story, but we see much of what Dick intended as the foundation of his fiction. Quaid's wife, Lori (Sharon Stone), as we might suspect from the original story, is indeed a government agent, her marriage to Quaid nothing more than a memory implanted a few months ago. His whole life, spent mostly dreaming about Mars, is, she tells him, just a dream. Returning from his treatment at Rekal, where he asks to be given the memory of his time on Mars as a secret agent and is consoled by the woman of his own choice (he asks that she be 'athletic, sleazy and brunette'; his wife is noticeably blonde), Lori tries to kill Quaid, but he escapes. Cohaagen (Ronny Cox), the grasping dictator of Mars, whose iron grip over its people is absolute, wants Quaid returned to him for new implantation. Meanwhile Quaid discovers a recording of Hauser, who claims that his identity has now been assumed by Quaid. Hauser instructs Quaid to get to Mars, check into the Hilton and, ultimately, to obliterate Cohaagen.

On Mars, the people are in effect serfs to Cohaagen, who has control of the air supply system, but the suppressed people have their own saviour, the resistance leader Kuato, whose identity is closely guarded, and unknown to Cohaagen and his men. Kuato needs to know what information is in Quaid's mind. At the Hilton, Quaid is left an instruction to visit 'The Last Resort' and 'ask for Melina'.

Quaid is taken to Venusville by a friendly black cab-driver, Benny (Mel Johnson, Jnr), and tracks down Melina (Rachel Ticotin), who must be the brunette that Quaid had stipulated in his dreams. Unfortunately she recognizes Quaid as Hauser, who had been her lover, and whom she believed was tortured to death by Cohaagen. She accuses Quaid of working for Cohaagen and of using her to infiltrate the resistance.

Cohaagen's response to Quaid's arrival on Mars is brutal. Unless the people give Quaid up to him, the air supply will be turned off and the population will die. Quaid is told by one of the captains of the resistance, George (Marshall Bell), that Kuato wants to speak to him. Kuato emerges from George's belly, a mutant creature of terrible ugliness but great goodness. Soon they are interrupted by Cohaagen's men, the treacherous Benny among them, and George is killed. Before Kuato dies, he tells Quaid to start up the half-a-million-years-old reactor that Cohaagen is guarding from the people – the reactor that will for once and all answer the problem of air supply on Mars.

The captured Quaid and Melina now see Cohaagen and Hauser

smilingly inform them that Hauser had volunteered to become Quaid in order to lead Cohaagen to Kuato's den. Quaid congratulates Hauser ('it's the best mind-fuck yet') and Hauser briskly tells Quaid that he now wants his body back. Quaid and Melina are strapped into restraining chairs for their treatment, as the people of Mars slowly suffocate. Quaid and Melina break free and reach the reactor, killing off Cohaagen's henchmen as they make their way. Cohaagen, terrified of the chemical reaction that will result from Quaid's interference, tells Quaid the whole thing has been 'a stupid dream'. Melina kills Cohaagen. The reactor does its work, hurling Quaid, Melina and Cohaagen into the vacuum of space; their bodies begin to explode. There is better news on Mars, where air begins to flow and happiness returns. A fully restored Quaid and Melina stare out over the stretches of Mars and wonder if, indeed, it has all been a dream.

'With this story,' said Arnold, 'I had to read through the last page to know the whole thing. I liked the dream-reality confusion. I thought audiences in this country and all over the world could be entertained by it visually, by the suspense story and its vision of the future.' This tells us a good deal about Arnold's understanding of this property in particular and his industry in general, in which success, artistic and commercial, is all-important. For Mario Kassar, Carolco's chairman, the success element was essential: 'Our pictures are designed for the whole international market as well as the US. They are attached to superstar actors, directors and writers. It's easy to lay off risk by selling off international foreign rights, country by country. That approach has worked for us, and we're sticking to it, even though every year such talent becomes more and more expensive.'

   In Arnold's case his agent Louis Pitt secured his client a fee of $10 million plus 15% of the gross, though Arnold signed no contract at the time the agreement was made; he has said it is his practice to sign contracts for his movies a year or so after they have been completed. The actual cost of *Total Recall* is debatable. Verhoeven gave a figure of $49 million while other estimates came in at $73 million.

The best talent in the business was becoming both more expensive and more influential, which was certainly the case with Arnold. His participation in the movie was not restricted to acting in it; he was also its prime hustler, barracking Columbia chief Peter Guber or Mike Medavoy of Tri-Star with demands for new initiatives or more money, and being the *deus ex machina* for ideas that others involved in making the movie had originated.

'I don't get involved in details,' explained Arnold. 'I sit in on the meetings and put my comments in there but I don't get that involved simply because I'm a director freak. For me the director is everything. I pay a lot of attention on who will direct because then I don't have to worry about this stuff.'

In fact, Arnold was effecting changes in his films that very few actors in an earlier age of Hollywood would have dreamed possible. It had always been a star's job to act. Being difficult had of course been almost a full-time occupation of many artists, and some influence might be wrought that way, but such overall involvement with every aspect of a movie was something quite rare. Clark Gable's influence over *Gone with the Wind*, Judy Garland's over *The Wizard of Oz*, was surely minimal; their contributions to the works were incalculable, but they were not in any significant way able to shape and demand the outcome of the work they were engaged in. Their philosophies counted for little. There would have been another actor to replace Gable if his ideas had crossed those of the studio, and Betty Hutton knew that even Garland could be replaced if necessary.

Arnold is altogether a more difficult actor to replace, perhaps because he is a very special kind of performer without really being an actor. As such, Verhoeven thought *Total Recall* would take Arnold further than he had been before: 'If Arnold likes the director and he thinks he is doing a good job, then he supports him as I have never seen an actor do . . . I thought I could bring something out in Arnold that had never been shown on the screen with the exception of *Stay Hungry*, this vulnerability and normalness of being just a human being, not a hero or superstrength guy.'

Arnold is of course not the only actor to wield influence in Hollywood today; the place is full of actors who like to think they have such power. The comparison with Stallone is inevitable, for Stallone's career is littered with instances where his ideas and demands have, not always to his credit, influenced the movies he has appeared in. Arnold has never seemed nervous of sharing the responsibility for a movie with the director and creative personnel – provided he approves of them.

Creativity is particularly crucial in *Total Recall*, because Dick's story is so enlarged upon and the detail expanded. Much of the action takes place on Mars (in the original, after all, Quaid does not actually ever get there), and is consolidated or extended by state-of-the-art special effects. The delicacy of balancing the psychological intricacies of the screenplay with the imaginative science-fiction setting, was also obvious to Verhoeven: 'The movie always takes these walls of reality away, suddenly, and you see new walls, like the Russian dolls one inside the other. What intrigued me from a very personal level probably related to my fear of psychosis and my ability to be psychotic.'

Verhoeven was happier when he brought in writer Gary Goldman to work on the final draft screenplay delivered in 1985 by Ron Shusett and Dan O'Bannon. 'What Gary Goldman did,' explained Verhoeven, 'was find one basic device to include a mind-level – I would say a mind-fuck in fact, because it's all about mind-fucking – and as Arnold even says, "This is the best mind-fuck yet." '

Dick's fascination with muddling reality with fantasy is skilfully expanded, taking the film along new lines that seem to develop naturally. This is largely due to the writers. O'Bannon came to *Total Recall* with much experience of the genre, having already co-written *Dark Star* (1974) with John Carpenter, *Alien* (1979) with Shusett, and *Lifeforce* (1985).

But the final shape of the film, as we have seen, did not rest with the writers. O'Bannon was ultimately critical of some things that happened to his work, while he and Shusett argued about a suitable ending for the movie; Arnold supported Shusett's idea. Further down the line, special effects technician Rob Bottin was also highly influential in shaping what finally ended up on screen.

Coming to *Total Recall* after working on *Robocop* (for Verhoeven), and *The Witches of Eastwick*, Bottin was so crucial a player in the game that his ideas noticeably influenced the thrust of the film. His images are immediate and brilliant. There is his memorable creation of Dick's robotic cabby, wittily transformed into a dummy pastiche of the all-American 1930s garage attendant. Named Johnny Cab – apparently after a cat litter – he nevertheless comes across as a self-sufficient Archie Andrews-like doll. Bottin's other inventions include the splitting open of the woman's head encasing a disguised Quaid when he tries to escape detection at the airport. His most inspired creation, Kuato, is perfectly timed to inspire a sense of wonder and repulsion, only to be followed by the bulging, choking faces of Quaid, Melina and Cohaagen at the film's climax. By the time of *Total Recall*, Bottin was already being lined up as the director of several projects, a development welcomed by Verhoeven: 'As a director, he could really do something which has never been there before.'

Total Recall opened in the USA on 1 June 1990, and quickly became one of the greatest films of the season, taking $25 million in its first weekend. Arnold, as usual, was kept busy promoting the movie and granting interviews, at each of which the journalist had to sign a document agreeing that Wendy Leigh's unwanted biography would not be mentioned.

In his delightfully individual treatment of science fiction movies, *The Primal Screen*, John Brosnan singled out the star's achievement. 'Arnie is the celluloid equivalent of a black hole; just as the incredible mass of a black hole's singularity bends time and space around it, Big Arnie has a similar effect on any movie he's in – because of the sheer physicality of his screen presence the movie kind of wraps itself around him.' Kim Newman in *Empire* also appreciated the quality of Arnold's new vehicle. 'The film,' he wrote, 'keeps pulling the narrative rug from under you in thoroughly unexpected ways that exploit the paranoid nervousness that makes Dick . . . such an insightful and important writer.'

Trevor Willsmer wrote that 'What distinguishes (Arnold) from rivals like Stallone is not just his sense of humour (but) also his willingness to make films which subvert audience expectations . . . While most other stars are refining their screen persona, Arnie seems interested in expanding his in new directions, while never failing to deliver what an increasingly loyal audience demands of him . . . *Total Recall* is, to quote Quaid's vernacular, the best mind-fuck yet.'

So many are responsible for the quality of the work in the movie. Arnold's leading ladies make strong partners, Stone representing the forces of evil and Ticotin the forces of good. The other evil on hand is well developed by Cox's Cohaagen and by Michael Ironside as his slimy henchman. Other evil may be presented with more humour, such as the Rekal staff and the ill-meaning physician who comes to lure Quaid back to Rekal, while good is concentrated in the people of Mars, the three-breasted prostitute, the dwarfed girls, and the pitiable George, who has given up his body as sanctuary to the legendary Kuato. Every mood of the movie is beautifully pointed in a glimmering score by Jerry Goldsmith. The photography is excellent. Jefferson Dawn's make-up is crucially important in the creation of Mars' mutants. The sixty-six stunt men on the payroll pull off spectacular feats.

Yet there are questions we must ask of *Total Recall* that do not seem to get answered. We are never denied the opportunity to enjoy the dual importance of reality and invention on which the film is built, but some of the practicalities are simply swept aside. The business of the reactor, reactivated to facilitate Mars' air supply, is hackneyed and badly explained. Arnold had come across an ending very much like this in the deplorable *Red Sonja*, and better might have been expected from those involved in *Total Recall*. Why does Cohaagen presumably perish when pushed out of Mars, but Quaid and Melina survive? The simplistic answer, presumably, is that they are the hero and heroine, while Cohaagen is the villain. In the closing stages of the movie we have the sneaking suspicion that we have been handed something of a cop-out. The 'pinch me and see if I wake up' feeling that suddenly grips the film as it winds down is not worthy of a film that is regarded as a highly intelligent leader in its field.

A sudden switch to whimsy does not compensate for so much that has gone unexplained before, but this may be intentional. Perhaps it is meant that, when we last see them, Quaid and his lover are merely two space-suited beings standing on the threshold of space, their identity no longer of too much concern to us.

While there are quibbles, nothing major detracts from the very real achievement of *Total Recall*. As sheer entertainment it is a feast, suspending us in a world (two worlds if we count Earth and Mars) where nothing seems as we might expect it.

Across this divide, Arnold's presence is the most crucial component. Despite the considerable violence he delivers a performance totally without arrogance or any sense of force, where it would have been so easy to strut through the proceedings. Arnold allows the movie to develop around him, from his beginnings as a believably loving and gullible labourer to his emergence as the saviour of Mars. Some smart one-liners remind us that this is the Arnold we know and expect ('Consider this a divorce' he tells the treacherous Lori before killing her), but everything here is in sympathy with the general plan of the movie.

Total Recall is a prime example of the special qualities Arnold brings to cinema. The film might never have happened without him, and that, in Hollywood, is considerable power. There is little concern that an Oscar may be waiting for him; he is simply not that sort of actor. With Arnold the presence can be all, but here he brings more, a vulnerability, an ordinariness, a feeling that, despite the muscles and the money and the unassailable stardom, Arnold really is one straightforward guy. Underplaying and the fetching gaucheness he displays may not be to everybody's taste, and may even be standing in for an ability to act, but at the end of the day the result is effective.

Arnold's supermensch has proved himself to be naïve, vulnerable, and inarguably human, achieving it all without recourse to any other of the characters he has previously created for the cinema. With *Total Recall*, so much of the furniture that Arnold's persona might be expected to lug behind him is gone. What other actor could have managed such a feat?

12 On the Good Ship Lollipop

It was inevitable that Arnold would at some stage want to try his hand at directing, though it seemed at first as if he was not preparing to vie with such distinguished actor-directors as Woody Allen, Clint Eastwood, Kevin Costner or Robert Redford. These, however, are words that may have to be eaten. 'I am trying,' explained Arnold, 'to develop a directorial career the way I developed my acting career. You start small, and you work your way up slowly, step by step.'

The beginning was modest, a *Tales from the Crypt* episode for TV, later incorporated as one third of Volume III in a full-length movie format, among whose producers were Walter Hill and Joel Silver, both of whom had worked with Arnold in earlier days.

The Switch, jokily introduced by Arnold in a fleeting appearance, is a neatly-written, undemanding piece of nonsense about a wealthy old man, Carlton Webster (William Hickey), besotted with a pretty young woman, Linda (Kelly Preston). Not wanting her to love him only for his vast fortune, he pleads poverty, but is refused by the girl simply because his face is too aged. He consults a plastic surgeon, who refers him to a 'mad scientist' specialist, Dr Nostromo (Roy Brocksmith), who offers to give him the face of a handsome, virile young blade Hans (by the time the credits roll he has become Lance) played, with some wit, by Rick Rossovich. A still dissatisfied Linda now demands firstly a new torso and, lastly, a completely new lower half, all of which Hans happily donates in exchange for Webster's money. Completely rebuilt and especially proud of his fine young penis, a revivified Webster runs to propose to Linda, but is horrified to learn that she has all along been looking for a wealthy protector and has now married Hans, who of course looks exactly as Webster did at the beginning of the whole exercise.

There is no suspicion in *The Switch* that Arnold is about to become the Orson Welles of the 90s, but the film is well done, with some neat reminders of James Whale's Frankenstein movies and, for the wide-awake, some in-jokes about Arnold's industry. Complaining that his expertise with the knife goes unappreciated, Nostromo tells Webster that, in America, 'they call me Jonathan' – recalling the defaced plastic surgeon of *Arsenic and Old Lace*. It is not surprising that the story depends on the perfection of the male body (of which Rossovich offers a lithe, tongue-in-cheek example), accentuated here by the parade of iron-pumping beach boys. Throughout, Arnold goes for smiles, not shivers, and the gentleness of the humour is notable for the sure hand delivering it. *The Switch* may not be *The Magnificent Ambersons*, but it is never, being Arnold, negligible.

One producer who looked at it with interest was Stan Brooks, who immediately sent Arnold a re-write of *Christmas in Connecticut*, the 1945 Barbara Stanwyck vehicle originally directed by Peter Godfrey. Arnold loved the script, watched the old movie ('I felt that I can do better than that') and signed on as director of the new version, in which Dyan Cannon took Stanwyck's role, that of a hugely popular TV cook renowned for her famous offscreen marriage and family, who is in reality unmarried, childless and unable to boil an egg. Cannon was to be strongly supported by Tony Curtis as her producer and by Kris Kristofferson as the man who comes along to change everything for the better.

Arnold brought all the application and enthusiasm to the skills of directing that he brought to appearing before the cameras, often taking his daily cuts to Ivan Reitman for criticism and discussion. Reitman was impressed, and went on to put himself forward as producer for Arnold's next directorial assignment, a movie about the slave Anthony Burns, its screenplay written by Charles Fuller. Meanwhile, Arnold's efforts with *Christmas in Connecticut* found encouragement from many sources, including no less a fellow actor-director than Eastwood, who offered to swap rough cuts of his new movie, *Unforgiven*, with the new boy. When *Christmas in*

Connecticut premiered on TV in April 1992 it proved an altogether lighter confection than the original, but then Arnold had found Stanwyck's version 'much more a downer. I guess I don't like depressing stories.'

In 1990 it was not only Arnold's film successes that earned him respect and credibility; it was no doubt to a degree the thank you from George Bush for the considerable support Arnold had given his presidential campaign when, early that year, he was named as Chairman of the President's Council on Physical Fitness.

'Everybody said "Don't do it, it's too much of a headache." To all of a sudden to get involved with an empire – every decision you make you have ten lawyers, telling you "no, this can't be done, it's never been done" – to go and convince that machinery to do it, to me that was fascinating. That's what "stay hungry" is, that kind of edge.'

Arnold wasted no time in strenuously promoting his philosophy of good living through physical endeavour; no chairman could have taken his duties more seriously. He strode across the American news stations with a politically fashionable catch-phrase for his new assignment, 'Read my hips. No flab.' He travelled to every state in America, chaired summit conferences on physical fitness, went into schools to talk and promulgate his beliefs, took trouble to talk to children and young people about their worries and aspirations. At one stadium 50,000 turned out to see him. The cynical might say this was a way of publicizing himself and his latest movie, but Arnold never used his position as Bush's envoy to further his film career. There was also the fact that Arnold himself paid his staff's salaries, and spent large amounts of his own fortune making the Council on Physical Fitness work.

John Butterfield, the Council's executive director in Washington, confessed that 'The thing many of us find so sweet about him is that he doesn't forget he came from very humble beginnings . . . He is so thankful to be an American citizen, someone who has been given a tremendous opportunity to succeed, and he genuinely wants to give back to this country what he feels he owes it.'

Years after leaving behind the career in which he had been

lauded and adored as a body-builder, Arnold was still on his pinnacle, still somebody the plain honest American could look up to. He was the ultimately successful immigrant who had been enfolded in the arms of the Mother of the Free and who had made good. It did not matter that his screen image had, over the years, been linked with gross violence, that movies such as *The Terminator* might be accused of glamourizing the very sicknesses that so beset American society.

Arnold was found not guilty, not responsible for inciting his public to behave in the ways he often followed on screen. To a remarkable degree, he had mastered the ability to separate from the images his film career offered up. Arnold was Arnold.

Arnold's next project heartily ignored half of the age-old warning that an actor should never work with animals or children. As might be expected from such a perceptive filmmaker, he went through the hoops with accuracy and imagination. When it was done with, he explained away the film's box-office take of a (so the studio said) disappointing $85 million by blaming it on the critics' perception of what had been attempted.

To the casual onlooker, Arnold and his team had merely given his audience what they most expected – gross violence, brute force, and the unanswerable potency of might over wrong – and commingled it with a cutesey kindergarten personnel of tots who were always happy to show their teachers they knew all about penises and vaginas. With Arnold's involvement, *Kindergarten Cop* was turned from what might have been an embarrassing hotchpotch of overbearing schmaltz into something reasonably telling and relevant, and always vastly entertaining.

As Arnold put it, 'I have good and commercial taste. When I call the head of Universal and say "I love *Kindergarten Cop*", he knows I look at that film as an American and as a foreigner. I am a market guy and not just a performer. When people look at me as being powerful, they are looking at the package.'

The team surrounding Arnold now was headed by Ivan Reitman, who had earned Arnold's gratitude by bringing out his comic potential in *Twins*. In fact Reitman wasn't at first keen to do the movie, but Arnold persuaded him it should be done, and that he needed Reitman's expertise. Arnold's determination was strengthened by the fact that this was the sort of film he would have made as soon as he arrived in Hollywood if he had been in the position to do so. Realistically, making the transition from body-builder to screen personality to film actor, always building carefully on the image he knew to be essential, Arnold had used the years to progress, gradually to introduce those elements of personality he knew he could exploit.

Working so closely with children, Arnold's empathy with them would be exposed; without that sort of chemistry, the film would flounder. Faced with a whole classroom of them, he was a little disconcerted to find they knew him not only from the relatively innocent *Twins*, but from such movies as *The Terminator* and *Commando*. At times Arnold got by with the sort of practical joking that had sometimes earned him enemies in the adult world. He explained to one dewy-eyed youngster that the way to become a muscleman was to put his thumb in his mouth and blow hard (at least suggesting that Arnold did not commit the cardinal sin of talking down to his little co-stars).

Murray Salem's story was strengthened along the way to bring into sharper focus some of the more serious social issues that ran through the piece, so that what we end up with comes across at times as a politically correct American overview of divorce (which, if these children are to be believed, is almost standard behaviour in modern society), single parenthood, and the physical and emotional abuse meted out to the most helpless members of the great American family. The rosy view that might have been taken, through soft-focus photography and soupy music, is by no means avoided here, but the pill has retained some of its bitterness, and it is here that the movie works best.

The misuse of children is only one manifestation of *Kindergarten Cop*'s violence. Played alongside this is violence in the pursuit of justice. This aspect recalls Arnold's predicament in *Raw Deal*. Then there is the almost parodied violence, evil so thick and transparent that one could wipe it off, of the evil duo at the heart of the movie, the drug-dealing murdering Crisp and his beautifully-turned-out mother who, by no accident, describes herself to a fellow criminal as a fairy godmother (the sort, presumably, who hands out poisoned red apples).

The violence perpetrated by Arnold's character is the most interesting of the three, though on one level it seems to be a straightforward kill-first-and-ask-questions-later philosophy trans-formed, through his contact with kiddie culture, into an all-understanding man, a man whose attitudes to violence are per-ceptively altered by his unexpected emotional experiences.

This is pretty basically done. Not surprisingly Arnold's hero is a loner, with an estranged wife and a long-gone son. His father and his father before him were cops, he knows nothing else; he works undercover in the dirty streets of urban America, looking at the world through shades, a deep stubble thinning his thoughtful face and upholstered by the weaponry which he has learned to flaunt; he lives in what we are told is a dump, eating junk food, his life fully committed to the capture of the evil villain he has pursued for years.

Connoisseurs of Stallone's movies may detect here a significant resemblance to the misunderstood hero of *Cobra* – and the resem-blance does not end there. Like other Stallone characters, Arnold's hero is transformed, softened and fulfilled by the love of children (in Cobra's case, his son). The difference between the two treat-ments, however, is more pronounced than any similarities, for whereas Stallone's (often charming and defenceless) performance comes adrift in a sea of mawkishness, Arnold's effort contains the mawkishness. It may not always be very real or convincing, but the strength is there, and the result is a comedy that threatens to be a telling account of modern American suburbia. If the children some-times come across as pawns, perhaps nothing much more can be expected in a movie that attempts to be so much else.

The opening is Rambo-like, Terminator-like, with world-weary cop Kimble (Arnold) blasting and punching his way through to the capture of the drug-dealer Crisp (Richard Tyson). Crisp has killed a helpless young crook after learning from him the whereabouts of his wife and child, who have escaped with $3 million of Crisp's sav-ings. Crisp is clapped in jail, and when sassy policewoman Phoebe O'Hara (Pamela Reed) is sent to pose as a kindergarten cop in order to discover which child is Crisp Junior, Kimble is sent along to assist. O'Hara, constantly eating to feed a medical disorder, becomes bilious and does not recover in time for school; inevitably Kimble takes her place. He confesses to O'Hara, 'I have a son' – one of the film's most catching moments, and one that Arnold brings off perfectly. Confident that he will cope with kindergarten, Arnold tells her, 'They're six years old. How much trouble can they be?'

The answer, of course, is plenty, and the situation comes to a head when Kimble, unable to stand the chaos any longer, runs out of school and screams with frustration. He goes back into class to face his unruly brood accompanied by his pet ferret, who is an instant success. The ferret marks the turning of the corner in Kimble's relationship with the children. Gaining their confidence, Kimble does not forget that his mission is to find Crisp's child and his mother, and the effectively-placed red herrings keep the suspense moving as our suspicions shift from one child (and mother) to another. Along the way the vulnerability of children and the facts of parental desolation are highlighted and championed by our hero.

First he has to win his way into the hearts of his pupils, which he manages with a novel approach to discipline and teacher-pupil relations, later celebrated in a *Rocky*-like montage of striving, happy children being inspired by their new super-teacher. In contrast, the children spread out on the floor to relax as Kimble reads a story he remembers reading to his own son. Looking up and across at them all, laying peacefully as if asleep before him, he is moved beyond words. At such moments it is very difficult not to like *Kindergarten Cop*.

The plot moves easily on. Kimble is soon attracted to a pretty and apparently wealthy fellow-teacher, Joyce (Penelope Ann Miller), whose son Dominic is a pupil of Kimble's. When news comes through that the only witness to Crisp's crime has been murdered (presumably by Crisp's obliging mother), Crisp is released and Kimble and O'Hara recalled. Knowing time is running out and that Crisp will come to get his wife and child, Kimble confronts Joyce and confesses that he is a cop sent to find them. Angry and desperate, she tells him it is not money that Crisp wants, but Dominic. Crisp arrives at the school, introduces himself as a trusty parent to the headmistress, Miss Scholwski (Linda Hunt), and sets

fire to the premises, kidnapping Dominic, who rescues the ferret
and stuffs it into his clothes.

In a final confrontation, with Crisp holding his young son hos-
tage against his escape, Kimble kills Crisp, but is himself wounded.
He is about to be despatched by the stately and murderous Mrs
Eleanor Crisp (Carroll Baker) when O'Hara clubs her to the
ground. Kimble is taken to hospital, where O'Hara comes to visit,
confirming their true friendship. On crutches, Kimble returns to
the school and falls into Joyce's arms, to the screaming delight of
the children.

Kim Newman in the *Monthly Film Bulletin* thought *Kindergarten
Cop* 'inoffensively scrapes by on thin charm alone . . . Arnie miracu-
lously but unexpectedly turns from gruff kid-hater to dewy-eyed
superteacher' – an odd assessment, perhaps, for Arnold's transformation is surely the one thing that can be expected of this movie.
Roger Ebert appreciated the ability to make 'a slick entertainment
out of the improbable, the impossible, and Arnold Schwarzenegger',
and noted 'what genuine affection the public has for Schwarzenegger'.
Most personal notices for Arnold were warm and appreciative, con-
solidating the belief he had always had in the film, his belief that in
its attitude to the use of violence *Kindergarten Cop* allowed him to
strike a new note, one that would continue and strengthen in *Last
Action Hero*. 'It was one of the few times when I could look at a
movie of mine and say, I think that my performance was good. I
believed myself in it, and that's hard for me to do.'

The manipulation of the film's main theme, the attempt to mix
violence with what some may find a severe overdose of charm,
showed again that Arnold's image was always shifting. If Arnold
had to sacrifice memorable one-liners to the children (pressed about
his father, one of them explains that his daddy is a gynaecologist
and spends all day looking at vaginas), elsewhere there were missed
opportunities. Linda Hunt, one of Hollywood's most admirable
actresses, is burdened with a sadly underwritten role as the
headteacher. Some of the kindergarten antics make one wonder if
the writers had ever heard of Joyce Grenfell's English nursery
school pieces. There are moments when the sweetness is laid on
with a trowel, as in the nauseating kindergarten class presentation

of the Gettysburg Address, culminating in an overblown speech from Miss Scholwski and a standing ovation from grateful parents to the god-like new teacher of their offspring. Such cloying moments sit uneasily with other parts of the film, but despite trailers that suggested otherwise the movie is not really first choice for a kiddies' matinee.

13   A Force for Good

Terminator 2: Judgement Day had always been a sequel waiting to happen. Efforts had been made to sign Arnold up for follow-ups of *Commando* (abandoned) and *Predator* (*Predator 2* was released in 1990 with Danny Glover standing in for the disinterested original star), but only the possibility of going back to Cameron and Hurd's masterpiece appealed to him. 'Arnie was struck by the dramatic success of the [first] film,' said Cameron, 'and immediately wanted to make another one. But I was kind of lukewarm about the idea. I wanted to go off and do other films. And I did.'

The path to a sequel was not helped by the fact that James Cameron was no longer married to Gale Anne Hurd, who had taken part ownership of the movie property with her. Yet when the right moment arrived, the necessary elements, including the money, worked together to make the project possible.

A glance at the finances involved in the new venture tell a salutary tale of the value of money in Hollywood in 1989. It was claimed that the original *Terminator* film budget was the equivalent of the catering budget for the sequel. Rumour had it that *Terminator 2* had the distinction of being the first movie ever to overspend by $100 million. The entire budget for the first movie had been $6.4 million, only $400,000 less than Cameron's fee as director and writer for the second. It cost $5 million to wrest the rights from Hurd, another $5 million to get back the rights owned by Helmdale Films. Against all this, Arnold's supposed $15 million ($7 million's worth, it was said, in the form of a Gulfstream G-III jet) seems small fry; without him, after all, the whole thing would have been moribund. Without him, too, it would not have finished up as the most expensive picture ever to come out of Hollywood (even though records of spending, at this time, were being broken every other day); the eventual total came in around $88 to $100 million. As Arnold said when filming closed: 'This has to be a very expensive movie because of what we have shot for five and a half months. We have used technology that has never been used before, and everything is very sophisticated.'

This technology and sophistication included the special effects, which eclipsed anything even dreamed about at the time of *The Terminator*. George Lucas' Industrial Light and Magic organization was brought in to achieve the stunning visual feel that Cameron envisaged for the movie, along with Stan Winston, who had worked his own magic for the first film and had also come up with the monster in *Predator*. The tight schedule that Cameron was forced to work within (the movie was slated for a July release in the USA) made the difficulties of using such wizardry seem almost insurmountable, not least because it would require so much post-production. Cameron tackled this by closing down filming at the end of every week and using his weekends to post-produce as he went along, thus probably making a Herculean task just a little lighter.

Many of the brilliant effects stemmed from the fact that the evil Terminator (replacing Arnold's original evil Terminator) is made of liquid metal, with the ability to transform into other beings and shapes, an idea Cameron had dreamed up for the first movie. The paltry budget, and the fact that no special effects team could be found to come up with the goods, resulted in Cameron having to fall back in the first film on a Terminator who was almost clockwork, and certainly hopelessly rudimentary compared to the more recent model.

Defying the fate of so many sequels to be so much less of an event than their predecessors, *Terminator 2*'s linchpin was of course the director, who had not been idle since the 1984 movie. He had followed up with a co-writing credit (with Stallone, no less) for the 1985 *Rambo: First Blood Part II*, a considerably potent film from whose politics Cameron ultimately distanced himself, saying the politics were Stallone's, not his. For *Aliens* (1986) he was director and writer, from his own story, followed by the less successful *The Abyss* (1989) as writer-director.

These last two movies relied heavily on their special effects, for which Cameron had an obvious fondness and understanding. In *Terminator 2*, 'the first action movie advocating world peace' according to Cameron, the director's lust for such effects underpin the whole thing. Even if it had had the worst script ever allowed through rewrites, even if it had contained the most damnable performances known to cinemagoers, *Terminator 2* would still be a film worthy of close and serious study because of the dazzling Pandora's box of magic that keeps opening up before us. As it happens, this is a movie that offers a very great deal more than mere technical brilliance, and what mattered to most people was that it had Arnold's name up on the marquee.

'I read the script on the way to Cannes,' he explained, 'and I was pleased with the twist and the idea of making the Terminator not kill anybody and become more of a human being. It added a great touch of sensitivity and sweetness to the movie.' There lay the rub, for when the movie was announced it was assumed that Arnold would be repeating his original role, and Cameron had considered having Arnold play a dual role in the new film, both the good and bad Terminator. Sure enough, when the movie arrived he was again playing the Terminator, but this time around Arnold's (and Cameron's) perception was cunning enough to transform him into a good Terminator, thus accomplishing in one deft stroke something quite unusual in film history – a character previously seen as totally bad reincarnating as not necessarily totally good, but certainly not evil, and potentially the instrument by which the world will be saved. This immediately gave new life to a reawakening of the original movie, resisting the tendency for Arnold to give merely a repeat of his 1984 performance.

Being still a robot, there is inevitably a similarity between the two characterizations, but when it comes to the leading man *Terminator 2* demonstrates a considerable advance on its predecessor. The original has Arnold handing in a neat performance, creating a remarkable image mostly by his presence alone, eschewing all but a clutch of phrases, among which his 'I'll be back' line tells us all we need to know about the resolute nature of this particular cyborg.

Arnold has also said that much of the humour we find in *The Terminator* was up on screen almost by accident, whereas there is no mistaking the intentional role that humour has in *Terminator 2*. Cameron's innate understanding of what makes Arnold a stunning and cinematically unique personality, and how Arnold can best deliver what he has to offer, works beautifully, giving Arnold his most successful acting outing since Cameron had last worked alongside him.

Children's swings and roundabouts washed in flames make for a striking prelude. We first see Arnold in the naked, crouching pose that introduced him in *The Terminator*. Walking into a roadhouse, he takes a biker's garb, finally deciding on a pair of shades to complete his trendy image. Despite the inherent humour of this sequence, we don't yet know this is not the bad Terminator of old. The arrival of another, the T-1000 (Robert Patrick), soon clears up this misunderstanding, for T-1000 wastes no time in assuming the identity of a cop; the police motto 'to protect and to serve', emblazoned on his car, has a nice irony.

The T-1000 has one mission, to kill John Connor. His mother, Sarah (Linda Hamilton), languishes in a frightful mental institution presided over by Dr Silberman (Earl Boen), from a long line of untrustworthy movie psychiatrists. Convinced that Sarah's talk of Terminators and the holocaust to come are symptoms of her schizophrenia, Silberman decides to detain her further, and will not let her see her son. In frustration and anger Sarah attacks Silberman, and is taken to her cell and restrained; a fat warder eases up to her defenceless body and licks his way slowly across her face.

Meanwhile John escapes for a while from the foster parents he loathes to practice his skills at credit card fraud, but is warned by an accomplice that a cop (T-1000, of course) is out to get him. The two Terminators come face to face, each wanting John for their own purposes, but it is the good Terminator that prevails, rescuing John from death after a protracted truck and motorcycle chase. The Terminator tells John that, 35 years from now, John has programmed him to come to Earth to save his younger self, but this good samaritan Terminator is not so sophisticated as his evil counterpart, who is modelled of liquid metal, can turn himself into any person he wishes, and whose limbs can become knives. The point is proved when T-1000 turns himself into John's foster-mother (after killing her), who then stabs her husband.

John, now alone, is impressed by the Terminator's devotion, catching on to the fact that the Terminator will do anything John tells him. Disturbed by the Terminator's natural compulsion to terminate, John tells him, 'You just can't go around killing people', after which the Terminator obligingly shoots only to wound (unless faced by T-1000). John instructs the Terminator to help him free Sarah from the asylum, where they are again met by T-1000 in time for another confrontation. The Terminator urges Sarah to 'Come with me if you want to live' (Reese's plea to her in the original film).

At first unable to believe the good intentions of the Terminator, Sarah remains troubled by what fate has decreed, and insists they head south out of the city. John introduces his new companion to some old friends of Sarah's as Uncle Bob. The relationship between the machine and John blossoms, as the Terminator ('the more contact I have with humans the more I learn') becomes a sort of father-figure to the boy.

Sarah watches and approves, but is troubled by what the Terminator has told her of the future: research in progress by a professor, Miles Dyson (Joe Morton), will eventually lead to the invention of machines that will, through the establishment of Skynet, lead to the holocaust, which she now sees enacted in her mind's eye.

Sarah makes her way to Dyson's condominium, meaning to assassinate him and thus change the course of events. She manages to wound him but breaks down at the point when she is about to dispatch him at point blank range, at which opportune moment the Terminator and John arrive. The cyborg reveals his true nature to Dyson by stripping the flesh from his arm and displaying the metallic workings which Dyson recognizes from the remains of the original Terminator in his laboratory; the only other part remaining from the first machine is a crucial microchip. Dyson, made aware of the horrors that will follow from his research, takes Sarah, John and the Terminator to his laboratory to destroy the remains, but Dyson is killed in a massive explosion that wrecks the building.

John still has the arm and the microchip, but T-1000 is in hot pursuit. In what promises to be their last meeting, it seems that T-1000 is finished off by the Terminator, but globules of liquid metal slowly come together to reform him, and it is left to the Terminator to consign his enemy to oblivion in the terrible melting-pot of a vast foundry. We see the fearful death agonies of the thing, writhing into every shape it has assumed throughout its evil life. The chip and the arm are similarly consigned to the flames. Sarah and John think this means the end of all danger, but the Terminator points out that there is still one microchip remaining, inside his own head; he too must be destroyed. John tearfully pleads with him not to go, but the Terminator knows what must be done. He takes Sarah's hand in a last gesture of friendship, for it is she who must work the switch that will end his existence. His love for John is now absolute; as he is lowered into the furnace he does not take his eyes off the boy. The Terminator's last action is to give John and Sarah the thumbs-up sign, a last, moving evidence of the human understanding he has absorbed.

For Arnold to have merely repeated his original performance would have been a regression. What Arnold so skilfully realizes is the need to carry forward a crucial part of the public's awareness of Arnold blasting his way through an expectedly violent picture, as well as the need to assimilate the other, gentler aspects he has slowly accumulated throughout his career, and since *The Terminator*.

In *Terminator 2*, Arnold arrives on screen with the furniture of his past six years of image-building. The new role maximized Arnold's comedic talents as well as his relationship to children (as begun in *Commando* and exposed fully in *Kindergarten Cop*), and the belief that Arnold has transmuted from a self-seeking hunk into a caring, contributing member of American society, canonized by his Presidency of Mr Bush's health campaign. All this and more is built into Arnold's reappearance for *Terminator 2*. Wittily, our sympathies are even more engaged when we learn he is now the outmoded Terminator model, having been replaced by the far more advanced T-1000.

Taking on such goodness does not mean that Arnold is the hero of the new film; he is really a Horatio to John Connor's Hamlet, a facilitator rather than an achiever, a side-kick rather than the top guy, and always a buddy in this cleverly disguised buddy movie. The hero may in fact be John Connor (played with a terrific lack of precocity by the newcomer boy actor Edward Furlong), or John's mother (Linda Hamilton, repeating herself in a generally under-rated performance of huge breadth and vigour).

Together Connor and the friendly Terminator combine as a force for good against the outrageously persistent and unstoppable evil of the bad Terminator, played by Robert Patrick, pixie-eared and sculpturally clean-cut in an impressive career breakthrough. Cameron's conceit that this more highly engineered model in the Terminator range should be measured against the proved track record of Arnold's redundant version is only one of the myriad strands in a complex but highly defined movie.

A change of side from bad to good and the infusion of a strong comedy element is not all that the new role has to offer its leading man. The crucial difference is that he has now been programmed to respond to, and be influenced by, his human compatriots. Thus, the young Connor takes a real delight when he makes the cyborg stand on one leg. Eager to please and to learn, this Terminator wants to understand the emotions of his young master, wants to know what tears are, and obligingly takes on board the peppy catch-phrases that John teaches him. He is a machine capable of taking on human attributes, and this leads to the blossoming of a very real, passionate friendship with the boy (Cameron and Arnold cannot have got through life without seeing *E.T.*).

What unfolds is a father-son relationship, recognized and ac-cepted by Sarah, who sees that the machine will not hit her son or abuse him in any way, will not come home drunk. In a world gone insane, this Terminator is the best thing that could happen for her son, eclipsing anything that any of the previous men (excepting John's father, whom she clearly adored) have offered. Cameron never relents his tub-thumping against the institutions and per-verted mores of Sarah's (and our) society.

These politics vibrate throughout the film where, except for one ghastly glimpse of happy suburbia (John's bickering, loutish foster parents trapped in a stifling marriage), the movie is all downtown, trapped in a desolate, charmless, wiped-out America of motorways, tunnels, inhospitable back streets, dismal cafés, amusement arcades and clinically obscene mental institutions. Although we are told the apocalypse is just around the corner, it seems already to have happened.

Against this background of physical and spiritual corruption, a good Terminator is more than a breath of fresh air, he brings unalterable values and a moral stance back into play, a role slowly recognized by the learning Sarah. For Arnold to be so involved in making this concept work as successfully as it does shows the extent of the advance on his earlier movies. Arnold's reinvention, we can see, continues.

If we have to wait to be told about the film's politics, we learn them from Sarah, who has learned them the hard way. Ultimately, all she can do is turn her back on the society whose future she is now responsible for ensuring. Despite her colossal resource and determination, it is of course the Terminator of whom she is most afraid. Not unnaturally, when she comes face to face with an exact copy of the original machine, she is so terrified of the death that is bound to follow that she turns heel and runs back into the horror of the mental hospital from which she has been trying so desperately to escape.

Her realization that Arnold's Terminator has his heart (if he could have one) in the right place, and her reunion with her son, help Sarah a little way along the road of understanding and restored sanity. We then have the delight of watching Sarah's love for her son alter the axis of their relationship, with John often taking charge of a situation, pulling his mother back from going over the top, and at the same time tightening himself up for his future role as a world saviour. Always ahead of Sarah shines the certainty that that future can be altered by their actions.

That vision is not going to happen without the help of the visiting angel Terminator, however, and it is essential that we totally believe in him, warm to him, mourn his ultimate sacrifice. The opportunities offered to Arnold by the new role involve much more extensive dialogue than in the first movie. As for the comedy, nowhere (except possibly in *Twins* which was, after all, supposed to be a comedy), has Arnold been funnier. Technically his acting may not be outstanding, and he is certainly neither a farceur nor a memorably witty cinematic clown, but the sense of pastiche, particularly noticeable in the play of voice and eyes (and how Arnold uses them to good effect time and again here), is wonderfully effective, and achieved with enormous economy.

So skilful is the volte-face the Terminator undergoes between movies that, by the time it is halfway through, it seems the most natural of devices. It is as if Rambo had suddenly decided to throw in his lot with the enemies of the US government and turned his guns on the Green Berets, yet it works. The difference between villain and hero is breathtaking, though Cameron's perception of the movie was much wider. '*Terminator 2* empowers the individual,' he explained. 'It says that, no matter how inconsequential you may seem to others, or even to yourself, your individual existence may have great value in the future.'

Terminator 2's strong characters keep our interest throughout. If any of them can be said to be complex it is Sarah, with her struggle to free her own spirit and clear the way for her son to save the world, a woman now very far from the Virgin Mary-like creature of the first film. Linda Hamilton's preparation for the role was as gruelling as anything Arnold has ever put himself through to get ready for a movie. Her conviction was that she needed to live out the intervening years between Sarah's first movie existence and her second. If *The Terminator* had made demands on her resilience, *Terminator 2* was even tougher. She took lessons in judo, learned military tactics from a one-time Israeli commando, Uzi Gal, acted out terrorist scenarios and – as we see in the first glimpse we have of her – even pumped a little iron. Her own workout took three hours each day in a six-day week for several months leading up to the October 1990 shoot. 'I was drained physically and emotionally,' she admitted. 'I don't believe any women have done what I got to do in this film, in terms of just carrying it so far with my body. Not just muscle alone, but hauling myself around to the point where I lost my hearing and couldn't walk for three days.'

Alongside Sarah, the villainous Terminator and John are less complicated but still believable, and the delineation of minor characters (the cold-eyed Dr Silberman, the sluttish foster-parents, the gradually understanding Dyson) is always good in a screenplay that makes the work effective on any level. As well as being a wonderful sci-fi movie, it is also a movie about many things that strike deepest at the human heart.

It is also a great chase movie, not only with its vivid traffic chases, but in the chases the characters are constantly involved in. They spend most of the time chasing from one part of the film to another in what is essentially a highly choreographed film (strengthened, again, by the mechanical precision of the bad Terminator's style of running).

As well as throbbing with this momentum, *Terminator 2* throws up many memorable images: Arnold pulling a gun from a golden gift box filled with red roses, the roses trodden beneath his feet as he turns towards killing his adversary; the burning wheel that rolls out of the incinerated truck that has surely (yet not so) polished off the enemy; Arnold's dressing for the part, plucking the shades from the pocket of a convenient sleazeball. And even when the movie seems intent only on delivering violence and action, the score ingeniously provides a strong undercurrent of grim persistence; this music, even when things are at their hottest sounds as if it is, properly, in mourning for the happiness of the world. Everything persuades us that this is a very fine film and, as far as Arnold is concerned, an absolute advance on what has gone before. Arnold agreed: 'I have to say that I feel sorry for the movie industry in a way. Because, from this movie on, they're going to be screwed . . . This is it. This is the answer, and those poor studio executives are sitting out there trying to figure out how to top it.'

Terminator 2 opened in the USA on 3 July 1991 to enthusiastic notices, an enthusiasm shared by cinemagoers. Despite bringing in a mere $31 million in its first five days (less than had been managed by the previous year's much less startling *Batman*), business had perked up enough after ten days to bring in a respectable $100,418,814. Available figures show the movie eventually took over $485 million. Its UK opening was equally satisfactory; box-office records were broken when it took £2.6 million in its first three days.

East meets West as Arnold's iron-disciplined Russian cop comes to terms with James Belushi's easygoing slob of an American cop in Walter Hill's flavoursome *Red Heat*

The unlikeliest of twinned pairs, Arnold and Danny DeVito point a blaming finger at the creator of *Twins*, Ivan Reitman

The clothed, well-groomed, charmingly ingenuous star of *Kindergarten Cop* gives a hint of Arnold's constantly shifting and developing image

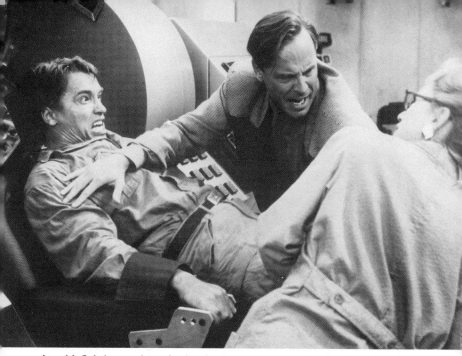

Arnold fighting against the implanting of an unreality in *Total Recall*, a thoroughly diverting and intelligent attempt in the science-fiction genre that proved a high-water mark in Arnold's career

A way with children: Arnold (with ferret) learning how to win friends and influence a new generation in *Kindergarten Cop*

Evil returns as Good for James Cameron's stunning *Terminator 2: Judgement Day*, reinforcing an image that pervaded our culture

Tony Rayns for *Sight and Sound* thought the film 'less a sequel to *The Terminator* than a benign revision of the earlier film . . . It represents another triumph for corporate film-making. What price the auteur in the days of five-minute credit-title sequences? Maybe the Academy should introduce a new Oscar for the Camerons, Burtons, Verhoevens and McTiernans of the New Hollywood: Best Ringmaster.' The intellectually searching *Sight and Sound* also carried the opinions of J. Hoberman who recognized that 'it is Arnold who seems the greatest of those extraterrestrial/immigrant/ supernatural strangers in paradise who have wandered through the movies of the past decade, validating America's suburbs and shopping malls . . . Proudly wasteful and bizarrely self-serving, *Terminator 2* suggests the merging of Schwarzenegger and Schwarzkopf. This is truly the Desert Storm of action flicks – mind boggling display of state of the art F/X angled at the international, as well as US, market.' James Cameron-Wilson for the *Virgin Film Review* considered it simply 'what cinema is all about; escapism, humour, action, state-of-the-art special effects that will blow your mind . . . Photography, music, editing, production design – all exceptional.'

Cameron now moved away from *Terminator 2* to begin thinking about his next venture, *The Crowded Mind*, utilizing a story about the problems of a multiple-personality disorder, saying that 'it'll be nice to be able to concentrate exclusively on the human elements involved'.

When Wendy Leigh's biography of Arnold surfaced in 1991, she sometimes found that her promotional appearances on television were suddenly cancelled. Fearing Arnold's displeasure and the possibility that he might resist appearing on particular programmes and channels, the television bosses had not been eager to let Miss Leigh air her views. The book's revelations clearly had little effect on Arnold's countless admirers, but then, as the *Sunday Telegraph* pointed out, 'in a crucial sense [Leigh] misses the point. With Arnold, it is not the facts that are important but the myths . . . Everything about him is larger than life. Or rather, other than life . . . He could easily be from another planet – the Planet Arnold.'

But Arnold was what he had always longed to be, an American, and a hugely powerful icon of his adopted country's popular culture. Leigh's account of Arnold's background got another kick in the teeth this same year when President Bush presented Arnold with the Simon Wiesenthal Center's National Leadership Award. As Bush said, 'He embodies the good, essential values of this world – values like caring and fairness and faith.' Arnold showed his commitment to peace (as distinct from the philosophies so often acted out in his work) by contributing $5 million to the Center's proposed Museum of Tolerance.

14   Ultimately, Arnold

In 1993 Arnold's career as a body-builder was still being celebrated when he was named as the best body-builder of his century (Aurelia had already been given her own award for her very individual contribution to the sport). There were other reasons for celebration, not least the birth of a new planet, Planet Hollywood, a new concept in theme restaurants stuffed with artefacts from famous movies, and not least from those of its three directors, Arnold, Stallone and Bruce Willis. In 1993 the trio came to Britain to open the London Planet Hollywood, having already launched the highly successful American equivalent. Wallowing in the opportunity to market his new business, Arnold was in his element, never missing the chance to do what came so naturally to him: sell himself and his concerns to the public.

Ivan Reitman may have said of Arnold that he is 'a throwback to the classic movie stars of the 1940s. If you're going to do it, why not do it all the way?', but Arnold's particular achievements surely leave most stars of earlier years at the gate. It was clear by 1993 that he also enjoyed what many in Hollywood would love to know the secret of – a happy marriage. Public glimpses of Arnold with Maria and their two daughters, Katherine Eunice aged three and Christina Aurelia aged one and a half, suggested that Arnold was making a happier childhood for his children than Gustav had made for his sons.

Last Action Hero, the sort of title that offers a gift to critics and headliners, was the Schwarzenegger event of 1993, and in many ways was a summation of the many idiosyncratic ingredients that go into the production of a Schwarzenegger product. It was also a testament to the fact that Arnold now unquestionably had what he had always sought, in life, in ambition, in Hollywood – an almost total power.

In the spring of 1992 Arnold saw it all in perspective: 'This run of success will end, it will, and of course one wonders what it will be like when that happens. But I am not the kind of person that thinks much about that. Right now I have joy with my family, joy with my work, and great joy with life. What else would I want?'

Some gossip columnists suggested that something Arnold might want very much was another, and final, career in politics. Arnold being Arnold, this could only mean one thing – the Presidency, but Arnold has always denied such ambitions and has seemed content to consolidate and manoeuvre his paramount role in world cinema. His marriage to Maria, ever free of any hint of scandal (another plus for Arnold against the all-too-public catastrophes of Stallone's unions), has not opened up any political dimension that was not already dominant in him. His and Maria's politics are still opposed, yet Arnold has never been an outsider to his Kennedy in-laws. As one observer remarked, his marriage is proof that 'the locker-room manners, the rough jokes, can be papered over like a rugger bugger at a Rotary lunch'.

Since his early days of womanizing, Arnold's attitude to women seems to have undergone a sea-change; he has a respect and appreciation of the opposite sex, though there remains the feeling that at least some of his views have a politically correct, fashionable quality. This does not mean his views are not genuine. His interest extended to visiting women's prisons. In 1987 he made a two-hour visit to a high security penitentiary for women in Frontera, California, talking, weightlifting, joking, signing autographs, encouraging, teasing. The superintendent reported that the prisoners had been surprised to find him 'sort of short'.

That same year Stallone was planning to open an all-male club, and tried to enlist Arnold's support. Arnold would not lend his name to the idea, pointing out that these were highly sensitive days for women's issues and that such an all-male enclave 'would offend every smart woman in the country'. Arnold's sensitivity was tested in other matters. He confessed that he was slightly unnerved when young children approached him and asked him to say 'Fuck you, asshole', at least proving they had seen him in *Total Recall*. If Arnold wanted proof of the power of his work he might have had more pleasant evidence.

Cannily, Arnold's confession came at a time when Hollywood was looking hard at itself, not so much at its track-record of sexually explicit and violent movies that had been flooding the market successfully for years, as at the evidence suggesting that more money might be made out of films that evinced 'family values'. Such pictures, went the story, would accentuate the clean-cut, homespun adventures of life and, more importantly, get themselves a PG-13 rating, opening the floodgates to family viewing. Suddenly, by 1993, every studio prayed nightly for the spirit of Walt Disney to descend and inspire, for here was a trend in moral perception, accentuated by the political stirrings fuelled by Bush and Quayle, that Hollywood simply could not afford to buck.

Arnold, of course, was perfectly placed to take advantage of this new fashion, this new insistence on decency and good, and his new movie clearly showed him able to mix and manipulate all those elements. For the man whose movies had grossed over one billion dollars during the 1980s, it was a challenge he could surely rise to.

The path to the new picture was strewn with forlorn projects. In mid-1991 Arnold was said to be working on a projected comedy movie titled *Jung and Freud*, with him playing Jung opposite the Freud of Dustin Hoffman. By May 1992 came the offer of the title role in a movie based on another comic-book hero, Judge Dredd. Arnold had laid it on the line to its producers: 'you can either do this excellently with me, or do it badly without'. A budget in excess of $50 million was promised, but several directors passed on the project and Arnold eventually turned it aside.

A remake of *The Count of Monte Cristo*, which might have been a feast of family fun, fell by the wayside (Arnold felt his accent ruled it out, but it had never stopped him taking on something he passionately wanted to do before). Other casualties, or movies that had to fall back in the queue, were Joel Silver's projected *Sgt Rock*, Ivan Reitman's *Oh Baby* and *Sweet Tooth*. The last, with Arnold promisingly appearing as a Tooth Fairy, might have broken new ground, and looked as if it might get past the winning-post. A director, Ron Underwood, was signed up, but doubts about its script weakness slowed things up, and *Last Action Hero* became the new Arnold vehicle.

It had quite humble origins. Taking a leaf out of Arnold's book, two students fresh out of university reached for success with a screenplay called *Extremely Violent*, whose hero's catchphrase, 'Big mistake', even made it through to the final re-write. Zak Penn and Adam Leff's work was auctioned and recognized as a promising Schwarzenegger vehicle but, in inevitable Hollywood fashion, it had to be developed.

Shane Black, veteran of the screenplays for *Lethal Weapon* and *The Last Boy Scout* (a possibly underrated Bruce Willis effort) was wheeled in to work on Penn and Leff's original, and decided to work in tandem with a colleague, David Arnott, whose *The Adventures of Ford Fairlane* was his sole credit.

The couple were put on the Columbia payroll for $1 million, eventually coming up with a draft that was convincing enough for Arnold to feel it needed even more work. William Goldman, a tried and tested doctor of movie-scripts, was then offered $1 million for agreeing to undertake a month-long reworking of the Black-Arnott effort. If there could be any doubt of it, the days when a pristine screenplay found its way straight from the typewriter to the production floor were truly over. Pleased with Goldman's surgery, Arnold appreciated the loss of some dubious humour from the earlier drafts and the fact that Goldman had brought out an essential and commercially potent closeness between the two leading protagonists.

Nothing was too much trouble for Columbia, who had won their industry's greatest possible prize, Arnold Schwarzenegger. The new head of the studio, Mark Canton, had since his arrival in late 1991 realized that his studio's future rested with the indisputably most successful star in the business. Coming together for *Last Action Hero* was a real meeting of strengths, in an arrangement that allowed Arnold more blatant control than he had ever enjoyed before.

For the first time, Arnold said, he felt utterly relaxed in what he was doing, confident that his use of power over the whole project had been contractually agreed on. Such power did not come cheap, with Arnold's $15 million buttressed by a percentage of the profits, but the studio may, with some justification, have felt that the price was reasonable, including as it did their leading man's involvement in every aspect of the film. Such control extended naturally to Arnold's concern for screenplay, casting, posters. spin-off products and the company's distribution plan for the movie. Guided by Arnold's bold and proven belief that the only way ahead was to 'start wide, get bigger, expand further and never look back' (a dictum that had worked for Arnold in body-building, movies and life), Columbia's confidence was high.

Arnold was as responsible as any studio employee for deciding that the new movie would bear its imprint as a more socially conscious film for the mid-90s, where violence, if not eschewed, would be somehow transformed, transmuted into something patently wasteful, evil, absurd, impotent. Money, not a sudden surge of moral sensibility, suggested this new thrust, when the studios discovered that PG-rated pictures were three times more likely to reach the $100 million mark than R-rated movies – and money talked. Canton reassuringly said 'Family entertainment without blood can have an edge, and you don't need blood or gore to have a good action movie.' (Had Canton suddenly become aware of some of the great films made by his industry generations before that seemed already to have made his point for him?)

Canton was almost certainly looking over his shoulder at Steven Spielberg's *Jurassic Park*, a movie to be unveiled during the same season as Arnold's offering and guaranteed to bring in family customers by the coachload. Perhaps a perfect solution would have been for Spielberg to sign up Arnold for *Jurassic Park*, but this would never have worked; in Spielberg's movies the characters and actors are of subsidiary interest – the format could not have made room for the Arnold persona.

Meanwhile, over at Tri-Star, Stallone's *Cliffhanger* (another gift of a title to those wanting to point out that its star's career hung by its own thread) was yet another attempt to rescue his flagging ratings. Worryingly, Stallone had once more done what he had failed to resist doing in the past: take the screenplay home and alter it. Arnold's skills had been in letting his personality permeate whatever project he was involved in, and in matching the best writers to the best scripts; what began to look like Stallone's constant error was not to leave some matters to those who understood better.

It was clear that in the 1993 stakes Arnold's contribution was now so individual and strong as to enable him to stand aside and apart, the most potent film image of his generation. And Arnold knew that image must change. 'The country is going in an anti-violence direction,' he said. 'I think America has seen now enough of what violence has done in the cities.'

These may seem grand words from the actor whose movies have promulgated violence, gross destruction and killing on a pretty magnificent scale, but there seems little reason to doubt that Arnold speaks as an intelligent surveyor of the modern world as much as a businessman. *Last Action Hero* is a surprisingly subtle stroke, opening a new debate on Hollywood's attitude to the society it reflects. The trick of the movie is to show scenes of violence only to have them questioned and ridiculed as the movie shifts its ground.

Using the movie-within-a-movie technique, this 'contained' movie distances its violent excesses; the violence on the screen inside the screen is ripe for parody, but is clearly itself a candidate for misunderstanding. Arnold's insistence that the days of Rambo-like annihilation are over is strong. Time will prove if this is merely a fashionable thrust, but Arnold vetoed the toy machine-guns firing toy bullets suggested by the manufacturers as necessary accoutrements for the Jack Slater all-action doll. As moral stances go, this is at least a beginning. As for the movie, it may be that in *Last Action Hero* we are watching Arnold beginning to transform the very genre he has done so much to solidify.

John McTiernan, fondly remembered by Arnold for providing a pleasant and successful experience with *Predator*, was brought in as director, presiding over a stipulated $60 million budget, more realistically rumoured to have reached $80 million. The task before him was prodigious, with a time-scale that would have spelled trouble for many a lesser director; a mere eight weeks of pre-production was followed by a five-month shoot and ten weeks of post-production.

Compared with this, the undoubted rigours of *Predator* must have faded into insignificance, emphasized by the fact that the omnipotent Arnold was now a great deal further up the Hollywood ladder than he had been then.

Arnold had always welcomed the thought of working with McTiernan again, and McTiernan repaid that welcome by relishing the possibilities of the new screenplay, managing even to sound rather as if he was Paul Verhoeven enthusing about the intricacies of *Total Recall*. 'When Slater's out of the movie,' he pondered, 'does that mean he's out of everything in the movie? Does it mean he's only out of the movie when the projector's running? There's a million mechanical questions you do not want to raise, because it would blow the fairy tale completely. You've got to find a way through them so you can achieve the effect you're trying to get without stepping in dog-doo on the way.'

An air of celebration surrounded the picture, with Maria making her début and guest appearances from Sharon Stone and Robert Patrick (both obliging Arnold by helping him bring off a considerable in-joke), muscle-hero Jean-Claude Damme (safely successful but not likely to present a real threat to Arnold's position), and Chevy Chase. Danny DeVito contributed the voice of a cat; Joan Plowright, a grand dame of the English theatre, made a rare trip to Hollywood to play opposite a leading man who must have seemed light years away from any actors she had worked with before.

As it turned out, *Last Action Hero* was hardly the most distinguished piece of work of her august career, and when the movie was finally revealed in America the critical reception suggested that for Arnold himself time might well be running out. If the writing was not on the wall, the wall was at last available for writing on.

What are we to make of *Last Action Hero*, a piece of work, an amazing conceit of opportunistic posturing, that must surely stretch the patience of the most devoted of Arnold's admirers?

Over the years we have forgiven Arnold so much. We have argued with his detractors that his work is so much better than those unfamiliar with it might suspect; we have accepted the fact that he long ago traded in any attempts at an Oscar-winning performance for that presence that has stood in the stead of solid acting; we have patiently noted the mordant wit that undercut many of the scenes of gross violence and helped expiate them; we have appreciated the fact that here is an actor who has made a very real, individual and highly-coloured contribution to our cinema and our culture. Coming to an understanding of *Last Action Hero* may be altogether harder, for there is a very real way in which the movie takes the scales from our eyes; we are watching a trusted conjuror doing a trick and, for the first time, not only do we see how the trick is worked, but we are forced to admit that the trick has not worked.

How promising and witty it may have looked on paper, this story of a bright, faintly troubled, freckled boy (Danny), trying to be a good son in his one-parent family, who loses himself in fantasy at a run-down, defunct cinema once run by crusty old Nick. Nick still shows movies – that is to say, the 'Jack Slater' movies starring one Arnold Schwarzenegger – to his audience of one, Danny, whose belief and trust in the capabilities of Jack Slater are absolute. Nick gives Danny a magic ticket once owned by Harry Houdini, and by its special powers Danny is transported through the screen into the on-screen Jack Slater adventure.

Lost in the fantasy world where Jack reigns supreme, Danny's eyes, at least as far as Hollywood's mores are concerned, are opened. When he again jumps out of the movie, accompanied by Jack, it is the adult hero who realizes that real life is lived in a very different way from his on-screen existence. Violence, he discovers, hurts and kills; feelings can be upset; other people have to be considered; the traffic will not stop when Jack decrees it should. Coming into the real world, Jack is chastened and improved by the knowledge that reality is nicer, more homely, than his screen life, and we are handed the message back, a great parcel of magic and wonder from our Arnold, who is suddenly revealed as vulnerable.

To any half-sensitive soul, the greatest noise of this movie is of those who made it having their cake and eating it. How brilliant a device, and how artless, to contain the scenes of violence (which are not inconsiderable, with, along the way, a truly insomnia-inducing murderer of quite ghastly ugliness, and a mugging of Danny that disturbs) in the story within the story, for in this way the killing and mayhem is worked in and pushed aside, explained away by being in the fantasy film-within-the-film. And when Arnold is seen in his most destructive, Terminator-like, guise, this is only Arnold pretending to be Jack Slater and, heaven help us, preparing us for later scenes where Arnold plays Arnold, arriving at a première for Jack's new movie and getting told off by Maria Shriver for promoting the Planet Hollywood restaurants.

A device that just might, with sensitive writing, casting, directing and acting, have worked, stumbles and collapses in a miasma of misfiring humour, where Arnold's latest catchphrase, 'Big mistake', sounds its own warning about the entertainment he has laid before us. Joan Plowright embarrasses us with an eminently unfunny introduction to Laurence Olivier's *Hamlet* (an in-joke falling particularly flat for those who know she was Olivier's wife), and a farting corpse (despite appearing in one of the best choreographed sequences of the film) fails to amuse.

Charles Dance's villain, with his collection of designer-glass-eyes, is little more than a left-over from a James Bond extravaganza, providing that sort of overdone nastiness that is guaranteed not to be taken too seriously. He cannot resist alluding to the characters of the film-world he and Jack Slater inhabit, as we wade through this collision between the milieu of Oz and the world of rampantly violent movies that have rung Arnold's tills for as long as we have known him. But the ruby slippers may have lost their potency, for the magic simply refuses to work. When Danny makes his life-changing exit from the real world into the world of screen fantasy, we are simply given a blank screen to stare at. This is a hopeless gesture, as if cinema, the medium that can achieve any visual sensation, has given up on itself. In this one moment the power and truthfulness of the movie are fatally undermined, for it reveals itself as being in the hands of people who do not care enough about its message. As if this were not enough, the laughably treacly ending leads us seriously to question the sincerity of the enterprise. Ultimately the movie is just not clever enough, and fails dismally on the few occasions when it tries to be, as when Ian McKellen (in a wonderful cameo) steps out of *The Seventh Seal* to deliver a warning of death. When it starts philosophizing the film betrays a hopelessly simplistic attitude to itself and to the real world its audience inhabits. And isn't there a sense, too, in which the very fact that Arnold spends so much time sending up himself, his reputation, and the genre that has given him bread, actually betrays the self-importance he and his industry are obsessed with?

Little surprise, then, that the notices for *Last Action Hero* were almost unanimously dismal, and that Arnold found himself, after a seemingly unending reign of success, with a prize turkey of a movie, lost against the tidal wave of *Jurassic Park*. Now Arnold himself, Arnold the unconquerable, Arnold the champion, began to look like the real dinosaur, turning his back on his history in the movies, pointing insistently at the morals that good American citizens should live up to, in a world where Jack Slater promises that the best Danny can expect of life is his first divorce and premature ejaculation.

As Jack tells Danny in one of his most cogent moments, 'The world is what you make it' – a philosophy that may not be profound but that presumably helped to inspire *Last Action Hero*. The trouble with the film may be that we feel Arnold has seriously underrated our intelligence, that he should somehow have taken his admirers into his confidence with a bravura display of understatement, tact and real feeling, instead of substituting the phoney schmaltz we have to put up with as, all gears crunching, he attempts to change the direction of his career.

Despite all this, there remains a nagging feeling, as we walk away from the movie, that *Last Action Hero* may be Arnold's misunderstood masterpiece, that the boy who wanted no more than to go out into the world with a monkey and a stick will have his last laugh. If we have indeed seen the last of the great action heroes we could have been in no better company, but it would be foolish to draw any line under Arnold's career when his pre-eminence in Hollywood has been based on his ability to learn, change and develop.

Perhaps *Last Action Hero*, determined as it is to show us a little of the real pain of the world, will ultimately strengthen his position as an icon for our age. Perhaps Arnold is about to become the conscience of us all. Having killed off the action hero, it is now up to Arnold to reinvent himself, to walk again into some new landscape of our imagination. For a man whose role models include Jesus of Nazareth, that may be quite possible.

Selective Bibliography

Ashley, Michael, *Who's Who in Horror and Fantasy Fiction* (Elm Tree Books, 1977)

Brosnan, John, *The Primal Screen: A History of Science Fiction Film* (Orbit, 1991)

Butler, George, *Arnold Schwarzenegger: A Portrait* (Simon and Schuster, 1990)

Callan, Michael Feeney, *Pink Goddess: The Jayne Mansfield Story* (W.H. Allen, 1986)

Gaines, Charles, and Butler, George, *Pumping Iron: The Art and Sport of Bodybuilding* (Sphere, 1977)

Kent, Nicolas, *Naked Hollywood: Money, Power and the Movies* (BBC, 1991)

Leigh, Wendy, *Arnold: An Unauthorised Biography* (Pelham Books, Stephen Greene Press, 1990)

Monaco, James, *The Encyclopedia of Film* (Virgin, 1992)

Peary, Danny, *Cult Movies: A Hundred Ways to Find the Reel Thing* (Vermilion, 1982)

———, Danny, *Cult Movies 3* (Sidgwick and Jackson, 1989)

———, Danny, *Guide for the Film Fanatic* (Simon and Schuster, 1987)

Robards, Brooks, *Arnold Schwarzenegger* (Magna, 1992)

Schwarzenegger, Arnold, and Hall, Douglas Kent, *Arnold: The Education of a Bodybuilder* (Simon and Schuster, 1977)

Woods, K.W., *Schwarzenegger: An Unauthorised Biography* (Publications International, 1991)

Filmography

HERCULES GOES BANANAS
(also known as **HERCULES IN NEW YORK**
and **HERCULES – THE MOVIE**)
1969. RAF Industries. 75 mins.

Director: Arthur A. Seidelman. *Producer*: Aubrey Wisberg. *Screenplay*: Aubrey Wisberg. *Photography*: Leo Lebowitz. *Production Design*: Perry Watkins. *Editor*: Donald Finamore. *Music*: John Balamos. *Leading players*: Arnold Strong, Arnold Stang, Deborah Loomis, James Karen, Ernest Graves, Tanny McDonald.

THE LONG GOODBYE
1973. Lion's Gate (United Artists). 111 mins.

Director: Robert Altman. *Producer*: Jerry Bick. *Screenplay*: Leigh Brackett from the novel by Raymond Chandler. *Photography*: Vilmos Zsigmond. *Editor*: Lou Lombardo. *Music*: John Williams. *Leading Players*: Elliott Gould (Philip Marlowe), Nina van Pallandt (Eileen Wade), Sterling Hayden (Roger Wade), Mark Rydell (Marty Augustine), Henry Gibson (Dr Verringer), David Arkin (Harry).

STAY HUNGRY
1976. Outov (United Artists). 102 mins.

Director: Bob Rafelson. *Producers*: Harold Schneider, Bob Rafelson. *Screenplay*: Charles Gaines, Bob Rafelson, from the novel by Gaines. *Photography*: Victor Kemper. *Production Design*: Toby Carr

Rafelson. *Editor*: John F. Link II. *Music*: Bruce Langhorne, Byron Berline. *Leading Players*: Jeff Bridges (Craig Blake), Sally Field (Mary Tate Farnsworth), Arnold Schwarzenegger (Joe Santo), R.G. Armstrong (Thor Erickson), Robert Englund (Franklin), Helena Kallianiotes (Anita), Roger E. Mosley (Newton).

PUMPING IRON

1976. White Mountain (Cinegate). 86 mins.

*Director*s: George Butler, Robert Fiore. *Producers*: George Butler, Jerome Gary. *Screenplay*: George Butler, based on the book by Charles Gaines and George Butler. *Photography*: Robert Fiore (South Africa), Robby Wald, Joan Churchill (San Francisco, New York, South Africa), Jerry Cotts (New York, South Africa), Robert Leacock (Holyoke, Mass.), John Karol (Los Angeles), Eric Darsfead (San Francisco), Jim Signorelli. *Editor*s: Larry Silk, Geof Bartz. *Music*: Michael Small. *Appearing as themselves*: Arnold Schwarzenegger, Louis Ferrigno, Matty Ferrigno, Victoria Ferrigno, Mike Katz, Franco Columbu, Ed Corney, Ken Waller, Serge Nubert.

THE VILLAIN
(GB: CACTUS JACK)

1979. Villian Co./Rastar (Columbia-EMI-Warner). 89 mins.

Director: Hal Needham. *Producer*: Mort Engelberg. *Screenplay*: Robert G. Kane. *Photography*: Bobby Byrne. *Production Design*: Carl Anderson. *Editor*: Walter Hannemann. *Music*: Bill Justis. *Leading Players*: Kirk Douglas ('Cactus Jack' Slade), Ann-Margret (Charming Jones), Arnold Schwarzenegger (Handsome Stranger), Paul Lynde (Nervous Elk), Foster Brooks (Bank Clerk), Jack Elam (Avery Simpson), Mel Tillis (Telegraph Agent), Ruth Buzzi (Damsel in Distress), Strother Martin (Parody Jones), Robert Tessier (Anxious Beaver).

THE JAYNE MANSFIELD STORY
(also known as JAYNE MANSFIELD: A SYMBOL OF THE 50s)

1981. Made for TV, Alan Landsburg. 100 mins.

Director: Dick Lowry. *Producers*: Linda Otto, Joan Barnett. *Screenplay*: Charles Dennis, Nancy Gayle. Adaptation by Stephen and Elinor Karpf. Based on the book *Jayne Mansfield and the American Fifties* by Martha Saxton. *Photography*: Paul Lohman. *Production Design*: Elayne Ceder. *Editor*: Corky Ehlers. *Music*: Jimmie Haskell. *Leading Players*: Loni Anderson (Jayne Mansfield), Arnold Schwarzenegger (Mickey Hargitay), G.D. Spradlin (Conway), Dave Shelley (Barry Charles), Laura Jacoby (Jayne Marie at age 6), Raymond Buktenica (Agent).

CONAN THE BARBARIAN

1981. Dino de Laurentiis/Edward R. Pressman (Fox). 129 mins.

Director: John Milius. *Producers*: Buzz Feitshans, Raffaella De Laurentiis. *Screenplay*: John Milius, Oliver Stone, based on characters created by Robert E. Howard. *Photography*: Duke Callaghan. *Production Design*: Ron Cobb. *Editor*: C. Timothy O'Meara. *Music*: Basil Poledouris. *Leading Players*: Arnold Schwarzenegger (Conan), James Earl Jones (Thulsa Doom), Max von Sydow (King Osric), Sandahl Bergman (Valeria), Ben Davidson (Rexor), Cassandra Gaviola (Witch), Gerry Lopez (Subotai), Mako (Wizard).

CONAN THE DESTROYER

1984. Dino De Laurentiis/Edward R. Pressman/Universal (UIP). 100 mins.

Director: Richard Fleischer. *Producer*: Raffaella De Laurentiis. *Screenplay*: Stanley Mann, from story by Roy Thomas and Gerry Conway, based on the character created by Robert E. Howard. *Photography*: Jack Cardiff. *Production Design*: Pier Luigi Basile. *Editor*: Frank J. Urioste. *Music*: Basil Poledouris. *Leading Players*: Arnold Schwarzenegger (Conan), Grace Jones (Zula), Wilt Chamberlain (Bombaata), Mako (Akiro), Tracey Walter (Malak), Olivia D'Abo (Princess Jehnna), Sarah Douglas (Queen Taramis), Jeff Corey (Grand Vizier), Ferdinand Mayne (The Leader).

THE TERMINATOR

1984. Cinema 84/Pacific Western/Orion. 107 mins.

Director; James Cameron. *Producer*: Gale Anne Hurd. *Screenplay*: James Cameron, Gale Anne Hurd. *Photography*: Adam Greenberg. *Production Design*: George Costello. *Editor*: Mark Goldblatt. *Music*: Brad Fiedel. *Leading Players*: Arnold Schwarzenegger (The Terminator), Michael Biehn (Kyle Reese), Linda Hamilton (Sarah Connor), Paul Winfield (Traxler), Lance Henriksen (Vukovich), Rick Rossovich (Matt), Bess Motta (Ginger), Earl Boen (Silberman).

RED SONJA

1985. Christian Ferry (MGM-United Artists). 89 mins.

Director: Richard Fleischer. *Producer*: Christian Ferry. *Screenplay*: Clive Exton, George Macdonald Fraser, based on characters created by Robert. E. Howard. *Photography*: Guiseppe Rotunno. *Production Design*: Danilo Donati. *Editor*: Frank J. Urioste. *Music*: Ennio Morricone. *Leading Players*: Arnold Schwarzenegger (Kalidor), Brigitte Nielsen (Red Sonja), Sandahl Bergman (Queen Gedren), Paul Smith (Falkon), Ernie Reyes Jnr (Tarn), Ronald Lacey (Ikol), Pat Roach (Brytag), Terry Richards (Djart), Janet Agren (Varna).

COMMANDO

1985. Fox/Silver pictures. 90 mins.

Director: Mark L. Lester. *Producer*: Joel Silver. *Screenplay*: Steven E. de Souza, from a story by Joseph Loeb III, Matthew Weisman, Souza. *Photography*: Matthew F. Leonetti. *Production Design*: John Vallone. *Editors*: Mark Goldblatt, John F. Link, Glenn Farr. *Music*: James Horner. *Leading Players*: Arnold Schwarzenegger (John Matrix), Rae Dawn Chong (Cindy), Dan Hedaya (General Arius), Vernon Wells (Bennett), James Olson (General Kirby), David Patrick Kelly (Sully), Alyssa Milano (Jenny), Bill Duke (Cooke), Drew Snyder (Lawson).

RAW DEAL

1986. Dino De Laurentiis/International Film Corporation (Fox). 105 mins.

Director: John Irvin. *Producer*: Martha Schumacher. *Screenplay*: Gary M. De Vore, Norman Wexler, from story by Luciano Vincenzoni, Sergio Donati. *Photography*: Alex Thomson. *Production Design*: Giorgio Postiglione. *Editor*: Anne V. Coates. *Music*: Tom Bahler and others. *Leading Players*: Arnold Schwarzenegger (Mark Kaminski), Kathryn Harrold (Monique), Darren McGavin (Harry Shannon), Sam Wanamaker (Luigi Patrovita), Paul Shenar (Rocca), Steven Hill (Lamanski), Joe Regalbuto (Daniel Baxter), Robert Davi (Max).

PREDATOR

1987. Gordon-Silver-Davis-American-American Entertainment Partners/Fox. 105 mins.

Director: John McTiernan. *Producers*: Lawrence Gordon, Joel Silver. John Davis. *Screenplay*: Jim Thomas, John Thomas. *Photography*: Donald McAlpine. *Production Design*: John Vallone. *Editors*: John F. Link, Mark Helfrich. *Music*: Alan Silvestri. *Leading Players*: Arnold Schwarzenegger (Major Alan 'Dutch' Schaefer), Carl Weathers (Dillon), Elpidia Carrillo (Anna), Bill Duke (Mac), Jesse Ventura (Sgt Blain), Sonny Landham (Billy), Richard Chaves (Poncho), R.G. Armstrong (Gen Phillips), Shane Black (Hawkins), Kevin Peter Hall (Predator).

THE RUNNING MAN

1987. Taft Entertainment/Keith Barish/Tri-Star (Rank). 100 mins.

Director: Paul Michael Glaser. *Producers*: Tim Zinnemann, George Linder. *Screenplay*: Steven E. de Souza, based on the novel *The Running Man* by Richard Bachman. *Photography*: Thomas Del Ruth. *Production Design*: Jack T. Collis. *Editors*: Mark Roy Warner, Edward A. Warschilka, John Wright. *Music*: Harold Faltermeyer. *Leading Players*: Arnold Schwarzenegger (Ben Richards), Maria Conchita Alonso (Amber Mendez), Richard Dawson (Damon Killian), Yaphet Kotto (Laughlin), Jim Brown (Fireball), Jesse Ventura (Captain Freedom), Erland Van Lidth (Dynamo), Marvin J. McIntyre (Weiss), Bernard Gus Rethwisch (Buzzsaw), Professor Toru Tanaka (Subzero), Mick Fleetwood (Mic), Dweezil Zappa (Stevie).

RED HEAT

1988. Tri-Star. 106 mins.

Director: Walter Hill. *Producers*: Walter Hill, Gordon Carroll. *Screenplay*: Harry Kleiner, Walter Hill, Troy Kennedy Martin. *Photography*: Matthew F. Leonetti. *Production Design*: John Vallone. *Editors*: Freeman Davies, Carmel Davies, Donn Aron. *Music*: James Horner. *Leading Players*: Arnold Schwarzenegger (Ivan Danko), James Belushi (Art Ridzik), Peter Boyle (Lou Donnelly), Ed O'Ross (Viktor Rostavili), Larry Fishburne (Lt Stobbs), Gina Gershon (Catherine Manzetti), Marjorie Bransfield (Waitress).

TWINS

1988. Universal. 107 mins.

Director/Producer: Ivan Reitman. *Screenplay*: William Davies, William Osborne, Timothy Harris, Herschel Weingrod. *Photography*: Andrzej Bartkowiak. *Production Design*: James D. Bissell. *Editors*: Sheldon Kahn, Donn Cambern. *Music*: Georges Delerue, Randy Edelman. *Leading Players*: Arnold Schwarzenegger (Julius Benedict), Danny DeVito (Vincent Benedict), Kelly Preston (Marnie Mason), Chloe Webb (Linda Mason), Bonnie Bartlett (Mary Ann Benedict), Marshall Bell (Webster), Trey Wilson (Beetroot McKinley), David Caruso (Al Greco), Hugh O'Brien (Granger).

TOTAL RECALL.

1990. Tri-Star. 109 mins.

Director: Paul Verhoeven. *Producers*: Buzz Feitshans, Ronald Shusett. *Screenplay*: Ronald Shusett, Dan O'Bannon, Gary Goldman, from the story 'We Can Remember It For You Wholesale' by Philip K. Dick. *Photography*: Jost Vacano. *Production Design*: William Sandell. *Editor*: Frank J. Urioste. *Music*: Jerry Goldsmith. *Leading Players*: Arnold Schwarzenegger (Quaid), Rachel Ticotin (Melina), Sharon Stone (Lori), Ronny Cox (Cohaagen), Michael Ironside (Richter), Marshall Bell (George/Kuato), Michael Champion (Helm), Mel Johnson Jnr (Benny), Roy Brocksmith (Dr Edgemar).

TALES FROM THE CRYPT: VOLUME III

1990. Warner Bros. 76 mins.

For *The Switch*, one of the three mini-films comprising this compilation, credits were as follows:

Director: Arnold Schwarzenegger. *Producer*: William Teitler. *Screenplay*: Richard Tuggle, Michael Taav, from stories originally published in *Tales from the Crypt*. *Photography*: Jost Vacano. *Production Design*: Steve Wolff. *Editor*: Stephen Semel. *Music*: Jay Ferguson. *Leading Players*: William Hickey (Carlton Webster), Rick Rossovich (Hans Dalton, credited as Lance Dalton), Kelly Preston (Linda), Roy Brocksmith (Dr Nostromo), Ian Abercrombie (Fulton), J. Patrick McNamara (Dr Thorne).

Arnold Schwarzenegger appears as himself introducing *The Switch*.

KINDERGARTEN COP

1990. Universal/Imagine Entertainment. 110 mins.

Director: Ivan Reitman. *Producers*: Ivan Reitman, Brian Grazer. *Screenplay*: Murray Salem, Herschel Weingrod, Timothy Harris, from story by Murray Salem. *Photography*: Michael Chapman. *Production Design*: Bruno Rubeo. *Editor*: Sheldon Kahn, Wendy Greene Bricmont. *Music*: Randy Edelman. *Leading Players*: Arnold Schwarzenegger (Kimble), Penelope Ann Miller (Joyce), Linda Hunt (Miss Scholwski), Richard Tyson (Crisp), Carroll Baker (Eleanor Crisp).

TERMINATOR 2: JUDGEMENT DAY

1991. Carolco/Guild. 136 mins.

Director/Producer: James Cameron. *Screenplay*: James Cameron, William Wisher. *Photography*: Adam Greenberg. *Production Design*: Joseph Nemec III. *Editors*: Conrad Buff, Mark Goldblatt, Richard A. Harris. *Music*: Brad Fiedel. *Leading Players*: Arnold Schwarzenegger (Terminator, model T-800), Linda Hamilton (Sarah Connor), Edward Furlong (John Connor), Robert Patrick (Terminator, model T-1000), Earl Boen (Dr Silberman), Joe Morton (Miles Dyson), S. Epatha Merkerson (Tarissa Dyson).

LAST ACTION HERO

1993. Columbia/Columbia TriStar. 131 mins.

Director: John McTiernan. *Producers*: Steve Roth, John McTiernan. *Screenplay*: Shane Black, David Arnott, from a story by Zak Penn, Adam Leff. *Photography*: Dean Semler. *Production Design*: Eugenio Zanetti. *Editor*: John Wright. *Music*: Michael Kamen. *Leading Players*: Arnold Schwarzenegger (Jack Slater), F. Murray Abraham (John Practice), Art Carney (Frank), Charles Dance (Benedict), Frank McRae (Dekker), Tom Noonan (Ripper), Robert Prosky (Nick), Anthony Quinn (Vivaldi), Mercedes Ruehl (Mom), Austin O'Brien (Danny), Ian McKellen (Death), Professor Toru Tanaka (Tough Asian Man), Joan Plowright (Teacher).

Index